Phil Esposito's
winning hockey
for beginners

Phil Esposito's winning hockey
for beginners

Phil Esposito with Dick Dew

Henry Regnery Company • Chicago

Library of Congress Cataloging in Publication Data

Esposito, Phil, 1942-
  Winning hockey for beginners.

  Includes index.
  SUMMARY: An introduction to the basic equipment and techniques for beginning hockey players.
  1. Hockey. [1. Hockey] I. Dew, Dick, joint author. II. Title.
GV847.E84   796.9'62   76-11204
ISBN 0-8092-8275-5
ISBN 0-8092-8048-5 pbk.

Copyright © 1976 by Phil Esposito and Dick Dew
All rights reserved.
Published by Henry Regnery Company
180 North Michigan Avenue, Chicago, Illinois 60601
Manufactured in the United States of America
Library of Congress Catalog Card Number:76-11204
International Standard Book Number: 0-8092-8275-5 (cloth)
                                             0-8092-8048-5 (paper)
Published simultaneously in Canada by
Beaverbooks
953 Dillingham Road
Pickering, Ontario L1W 1Z7
Canada

contents

	introduction	6
chapter one	history	8
chapter two	facilities and other considerations	12
chapter three	conditioning	20
chapter four	equipment	36
chapter five	carrying the puck	58
chapter six	shooting	64
chapter seven	checking	78
chapter eight	goaltending	88
chapter nine	face-offs	110
chapter ten	defense: a summary	120
chapter eleven	attitude	128
appendix I	the career of phil esposito	135
appendix II	diagrams	137
	glossary	147
	index	157

introduction

No matter how you treat and receive this book—whether you study it and do the things discussed in it or not—you should always remember this:

"You're only as good as the physical condition you're in and the state of mind you're in. Because if you think you're beaten, you are. If you think you dare not, you don't. If you'd like to win but you think you can't, it's almost a cinch you won't win. If you think you'll lose, you've lost for sure. For out in the world you find success begins with the fellow's will. It's all in the state of mind."

I read that somewhere and wrote it down. I don't know who wrote it but I like it, I believe it.

One other thing. I make reference throughout this book to male hockey players. However, I believe this book is just as applicable to girls as it is to boys. I think it would be good for girl players. And if

introduction

they want to play hockey, they should play hockey. Why shouldn't they? They do everything else, so why not? If a young lady of any age wants to learn how to play, I think it's beautiful, and I hope that this book will help her.

My experience in hockey schools is that girls, particularly at the younger ages, work just as hard as boys. So I hope this book will help the girls just as much as it does the boys.

chapter one

You might get a dissenting vote from the Soviet Union, but the game of ice hockey, as it is known today, began in Canada and emigrated from there in nearly all directions over the years.

Originally played with seven men on a side and with netless nets—two pipes hammered into the surface of an icy pond—the sport didn't really begin to flourish until around the turn of the century.

Hockey went professional early and had the first of several bidding wars just prior to World War I. The teams were shaved to six players in 1912.

Games were played in two 30-minute periods instead of the present three 20-minute (or less) sessions. Playoff series were decided on total goals rather than game victories.

It was a hop, a skip, and a few painful but lucrative player jumps

history

later that the demands of war sharply limited the top end of the sport, which dipped to a low of four pro teams in 1917.

The National Hockey League, which today considers itself both sire and dam of the sport, officially came into being with four teams, two of them from Montreal, in 1917.

The infant league struggled through an inaugural season during which one of its members went out of business. So two of the remaining three survivors played off for the championship trophy, called the Stanley Cup, which had originated back in 1893.

They were playing 18- and 22-game regular seasons in those days, a far cry from the current seasons, in which NHL teams can play nearly 100 exhibition, regular, and post-season games.

They were working steadily on the rules in those days, too, introducing much of the playing legislation that exists to this day. The war in Europe was long over, but hockey had a few memorable battles of its own to help speed the rule-writing process.

But despite their problems, two rival leagues (in the East and the West) were slowly getting bigger and stronger from a financial standpoint, and the game was earning ever-spreading acceptance.

The western segment, the Pacific Coast Hockey Association, spread into the United States with teams in Portland and Seattle; the four-team National Hockey League, the eastern branch of the family, made its move in 1924. The NHL added the Boston Bruins as a franchise and established New York as another expansion city for 1925.

League officials also expanded the schedule from 24 to 30 games, and that produced a brief player strike late in the season.

The success of the New York franchise opened the door to further U.S. expansion, Pittsburgh, Detroit, and Chicago moving in with players acquired from the defunct teams of the western league.

The NHL underwent frequent and drastic changes during the depression years and survived only to be hit by another world war, one that quickly put dozens of top stars into uniform.

Montreal's powerful Canadiens generally dominated the league during the postwar period. In 1967 the NHL undertook a massive expansion program, doubling its size with six new franchises.

They've done little juggling since then, leaving what is still billed as the most successful full-scale expansion in major pro sports history.

The NHL had the pro field to itself until 1972, when the World Hockey Association showed up, re-creating the bidding wars of 60 years earlier.

While the NHL was clearly showing the way over the years, hockey flourished as an amateur sport as well. It became an official event of the Olympic Games in 1920 and established its own world championship tournament four years later.

While junior hockey has always flourished in Canada, where it has been the prime supplier of young NHL talent, U.S. collegiate hockey programs have grown tremendously in the last few years, often by the simple expedient of recruiting young Canadian players.

history

The progress of the colleges and the expansion of the U.S. schoolboy programs can be measured in part by the fact that an increasing number of professionals are now coming from the college and school ranks.

The vastly different philosophies of sport in the East and the West finally led to a new aspect of hockey in 1972. NHL players, as professionals, rarely got a crack at the Russian teams, which had taken a stranglehold on Olympic and international competition on the basis of their amateur status.

An eight-game series between teams of selected professional stars from the NHL and the amateurs of the Soviet Union was finally arranged. It produced one of the more spectacular confrontations in the history of hockey.

Team Canada, a squad limited to Canadian nationals in the NHL, fell behind in the series on its home grounds and trailed, one win to three for the Soviets (with one tie), following the shift to Russia.

But Team Canada staged a fiction-like comeback in very hostile territory, Paul Henderson scoring the winning goal with 34 seconds remaining in the final game to give the NHL team the final edge, four wins to three with one tie. It was the rebound from my own shot that Henderson converted into the series winner.

I wound up as series scoring leader with seven goals and six assists. Then I won national acclaim in Canada after publicly chastising a relatively few fans who had berated Team Canada as it fell behind earlier in the series.

Competition between the professionals of the West and the amateurs of the East subsequently expanded to include players from the World Hockey Association and individual NHL teams.

Not surprisingly, the pros and the Russians have proven to be relatively well matched, and highly competitive, too. But no confrontation is ever likely to equal the drama of that first series.

chapter two

The big change and improvement in facilities, both in the United States and Canada—but particularly in the U.S.—is having a tremendous effect on hockey and hockey players.

When I was a youngster, we played on an open-air rink; to get it started we needed a snowstorm, six or even ten inches on the ground.

We'd all go out, the kids, their fathers, the fans, and pat it down with shovels and stomp the snow with our feet until it was a flat surface. Then, we'd get a hose and flood it again and again, walking backwards as we sprayed water every hour. We'd put in more snow to fill in the holes, flood it 10 or 15 times.

I can remember my father going out at midnight to flood an open-air rink for my brother Tony and me. In the morning, unless it snowed during the night, it would be great. I used to love flooding the rink, but I wasn't too happy when we had to plow it off.

facilities and other considerations

We had only one artificial rink when I was growing up, but with greatly improved freezing equipment and changing times there are many, many more now.

And the facilities are having an effect on the development of young hockey players, too. I think everyone knows that, with all the rinks that are being put up across the United States, more kids are playing hockey than ever before.

I think more Americans are going to be playing hockey in the NHL soon, very soon. There are more of them every year now.

I see definite improvement in the youngsters in the various hockey schools in which I am involved. I'm just amazed sometimes at kids 14 and 15 years old, how they can handle the puck.

The most important improvement that I've seen is in how they shoot. It amazes me that kids this age can shoot as hard as they can.

Another thing I see now is that kids are getting a lot bigger, too. When I first broke into hockey, I was a lot bigger than most of the other players. Now, I'm just an average size. Everything is changing.

It's probably only a matter of time before U.S. players catch up with Canadians as potential hockey professionals. I don't know when it will happen that they will be equals but I think it's coming. Maybe not while I'm still playing, but I think it is definitely going to come. I believe that eventually it will be pretty much uniform. I do feel that the coaching really leaves a lot to be desired in the United States.

I suspect it will be up to people like myself, who are going to continue to live in the United States when we're finished as players, to take a more active interest in the development, coaching, and improvement of the training of these kids.

I think that sooner or later U.S. boys are going to be on a par, equal footing, with Canadian kids. But there are going to have to be some changes first.

What happens now is that up to the age of 14 kids in the U.S. are just as good as, if not better than, Canadian boys. At least, that's what I find in the hockey schools.

But after 14, the coaching gets better in Canada. These kids have to play high school hockey in the U.S. I think they've got to change the rules, just let them go out and play.

I think they'll have to have a junior league in the U.S. soon. They'll have to form a junior program comparable to the Ontario Hockey Association in Canada.

I believe that sooner or later it's going to have to become widespread. I know they have some small programs operating on their own now. I know that Buffalo has been trying to get a junior franchise. If they get it, I know there may be a lot of Canadian kids in it. But I think sooner or later the U.S. has to come up with a comparable junior league or program.

I can't see why they don't do it now. There are a lot of guys capable of coaching, giving kids instruction at 14 and 15 years old. What happens now is that when they get to be 16 or 17 years old, if they want to play junior hockey, they've got to go up to Canada to play.

facilities

Who is to blame? I don't think it's the Canadians. It's the Americans, who establish youth programs and don't follow through on them. In Minnesota now, the schoolboy players can't even go to a hockey school run by a professional and continue to play high school hockey.

I not only don't think that's right, I think it is ridiculous. And it tends to expose some of the coaching in the high schools and even the colleges.

Some of these coaches might never have played a game of hockey in their lives, but they think they know it all. There is one thing that I have learned from playing this game, and that is that you never stop learning!

They put limits on the number of games boys can play. I know that when I was young, we used to play one game a week and practice once a week. And we'd crave all the time to play more.

Of course, I don't think kids should be playing every night. I don't believe in that. And I don't think they should be practicing every night.

You see, I don't believe that kids have to be organized into teams and leagues when they're eight and nine years old. I wasn't when I was that age. I just wanted to play hockey, by myself if necessary.

They should just go out and skate and play, on ice if it's available, or play street hockey if there's no ice. Why should a boy be put into a position at that age and try to learn that to the exclusion of anything else?

Who says they must have officials at that age? We learned to call offsides among ourselves. Sure, we'd argue or ask somebody. That's how we learned.

In my hockey schools, I want the players to tell me when there is an offside. That's the best way to learn what is and what isn't an offside, not just having somebody tell them all the time.

And of course playing hockey can be overdone, particularly at the younger ages. It's like anything else in life. If you get too much of it you can lose interest.

It does seem to me that the junior program in Canada has had one interesting side effect—U.S. college hockey has gotten a lot better than Canadian college hockey as a result. Canadian kids play junior hockey and after they're through there, they turn pro. But some kids get a choice, the option of going into college hockey.

I believe a youngster should go to school as long as he can and as long as he wants to. It's fine to combine hockey and education, as football and basketball do. And I think that more and more professional teams are getting their kids from college hockey all the time. So if a young man can combine his education and his hockey, great.

Not everyone can do that, not everyone is capable of going to college and having a hockey career at the same time. I think parents should realize that their youngsters might not be able to do that.

If a boy has a chance to turn professional hockey player, he has a decision to make. And neither I nor anybody else can make that decision for him.

If a decision is reached to play college hockey, where should a youngster go to school? Again, his decision. But there is more opportunity in college hockey in the U.S. than there is in Canada. Obviously, there are more college hockey teams in the U.S. and I understand the number is growing all the time.

There is more opportunity for a young Canadian boy in junior hockey than there is in college hockey. But you must remember that boys start playing junior hockey when they're in high school or even younger. That's when the decision has to be made.

Where practice is concerned, I think there should definitely be a limit to the amount of time young players spend in a regular practice or instructional program.

I believe that, nowadays, kids can play too much hockey. I think they can get fed up with it before they're 14 or 15 years old. I don't think you should ever be on the ice more than two hours at a time. I've decided that at our hockey schools even two hours in a shift is too much for the kids to handle.

Remember, age should have a bearing on this. An adult player might have the stamina for two hours but a youngster isn't likely to. I'd set two hours as the most time anyone should practice at a time and cut back from there depending on the age of the players involved.

For instance, in our own training camps, the pros usually go from 9 to 10:30 in the morning. Then we go back on the ice from 1 P.M. to

facilities

2:15. So you see we don't even do four hours a day, even in split shifts. I think if you're talking about split sessions, three hours a day should be the absolute top.

There is another aspect of playing hockey that I want to mention, and this seems as good a time as any. Lots of times fans, people who for the most part have never played hockey or played anything professionally, think that the athlete has a life of ease. They look at the schedule, for instance, and see that you play two or three games in a week and have several days off between games. They get the wrong impression from that because they don't stop to think about the lives we lead.

Sure, we get days off, but as a general rule the combination of games, practice, and travel takes up a lot more than the 35 or 40 hours a week that most people work these days.

I think the hardest thing is the travel: it's something that sooner or later is going to have to be changed and improved: The NHL travel rule, that you should almost always be in the city where you're playing your next game the day or night before that game is scheduled.

We all realize and accept the idea that if you're not careful with your travel plans, you can get grounded or locked in some place by bad weather or equipment failure or something like that.

Certainly, the fans who have bought the tickets—who pay our salaries—have a right to expect that we will be there, that the game will be played on time and as scheduled.

In the first place, nearly all the games are scheduled at night. And for economic reasons, most teams are now flying on regular commercial flights. Chartering is just too expensive.

After a game, no matter where it is played or who it is against, it takes me a good three hours to unwind, to settle myself down so I can go to sleep.

If we play on Saturday night in, say, Pittsburgh, we leave the next morning and play that night. But we don't get to sleep until two or three o'clock in the morning and we have to get up at five-thirty or six o'clock in the morning to get an early flight.

It's just plain too much, too exhausting. I don't know what they can do about it how they can correct it, but something is going to have to be done.

17

It's even more difficult if we have a Saturday night game someplace and have to be in another city for a Sunday afternoon game. There aren't many of those, but it takes me days to recover from a schedule like that.

There are a few times when we get a break from the scheduling. In Detroit, for instance, they play some Saturday afternoon games. So if we happen to be scheduled there, we can fly out in the early hour, and be in pretty good shape the next day, even if it happens to be an afternoon game.

I wish more teams in more cities could schedule Saturday afternoon games, but it doesn't seem to work out in a lot of places. Detroit is an exception. And you've got to do what the fans want; that's primary.

Aside from the sleeping problem, there's the matter of eating. An athlete should have a good, balanced diet. But how do you maintain a regular eating program under those circumstances?

I confess I can't answer the question but I know from experience that it isn't a problem for just those of us who are in the NHL. The problem exists all through hockey, at just about every level, whether you're traveling by bus or by jet. And I suppose much the same thing is true in other sports. At least, that's what I've often heard from other athletes.

I would like to say something about the rules. I believe they should be uniform, the same, in all levels of hockey. I don't necessarily mean that the National Hockey League should be able to dictate rules for everybody, amateur and professional alike.

And I don't see how international rules can be imposed on everybody, either. I know the NHL rules because I have to know them, that's how I make my living. And it would be pretty silly for me or any professional not to know the rules governing his own profession.

It seems to me that the ultimate goal of a youngster playing organized hockey is to reach the NHL, to make his living in hockey. So it makes no sense at all to me that he should run into different rules on different levels. It's tough enough to move up and break into a new and stronger league without having to change your play or your style to conform with a new set of rules.

To me, much of the difference in rules is political, men who want to create jobs for themselves. As far as I'm concerned, it's wrong. I really get upset when I hear about variations, things like eliminating icing. There are so many variations that it would be impossible to go into them.

As a general thing, I prefer the NHL rules, maybe because I'm so accustomed to them. And it seems to me that the various versions of the rules are slowly, very slowly, coming together.

There is one thing I encountered in the international rules that I would like to see written into the NHL rules. That's the matter of fighting. I believe that sooner or later, you'll have to adopt the rule that if you fight, you're out of the game. I like it—but with reservations. On the positive side, it would stop a lot of these guys who are always brawling.

But then it could create a situation where a coach could say, "Go out and get that guy out of the game." I don't know how you're going to control that.

As a general thing, I think too much is made about fighting and violence in hockey. The media overreacts and of course the fans do, too. And you get the political thing again, men trying to make a name for themselves by knocking hockey.

Now, mind you, I'm not a pacifist. I know that no set of rules can eliminate fighting. Hockey is, after all, a contact sport. It's rough and it's bound to result in some fighting.

As a professional player, I can take only so much and then I've got to fight back to some degree. If I don't, I'll be run right out of the league.

Players will come out and try to take advantage of you, they'll be all over you. Unless they know you're going to give it back to them to some extent, they'll run roughshod over you.

One area where I draw the line, and I think everybody should, is in the matter of sticks. They should never be used in a fight. I was there when Ted Green got very badly hurt some years ago. I saw Eddie Shack and Larry Zeidel have a terrible, terrible stick fight.

I don't think you should ever hit a player with a stick. It's just too dangerous; it's too easy to cause a very serious injury. I believe that if you get into a scramble with a guy, the sticks should go down immediately. It just isn't necessary. Most players feel that way.

chapter three

The most important thing for any hockey player—or any athlete in any sport or activity—is his physical condition. It's got to be obvious that a player in top shape is going to perform better than somebody who is out of shape.

And it's never made any sense at all to me to play a sport in anything less than good physical condition. If you're going to do something, why not try to do it the right way? And your physical condition is as basic as your equipment.

Now, you can get a lot of debate on the best method of physical conditioning. And I don't propose to lay out a whole lot of rules that will start an argument with anybody.

What I am saying is what I have found to be true for me personally, what I have learned over the years in getting myself into shape and keeping myself that way.

conditioning

I am, after all, a professional hockey player. But I won't be a professional hockey player very long if I don't take care of my body. For instance, what good would it do me if I worked out regularly but at the same time didn't get enough rest, or if I weren't careful with my diet?

To me, one area where I didn't take care of myself would offset another where I did do what I should, what I knew was right for me. So I'd be in effect wasting a lot of time and energy. And I don't believe in waste—and you can spell that *waist* if you want to.

That's my first point. I'm a pretty big guy, so obviously one of the things I have to watch is my weight. Sure, that's true for a little guy, too. But my point is that if you have a problem area, that's an area you should concentrate on.

For instance, after I had my knee operation a couple of years ago,

Use of the toe (tip of the skate blade) to get started in a kind of running motion.

Pushing off on the full blade of the skate in picking up speed.

it was obvious I had to build up the knee and the leg. The muscles in my leg had deteriorated badly while I was recuperating from the operation.

One of the things I did as soon as I could was a lot of special leg exercises and running. It took quite a while and it was no fun, but it paid off.

Now, remember, when I was concentrating on one area because of a particular problem, I had to remember at all times not to let any other physical problem develop.

Sure, running was good for my wind and stamina, but if I had been overeating and putting on too much weight while I was limited in my activities, I'd be making a ridiculous mistake.

As far as general exercise is concerned, it has always seemed to me that the best thing you can do is work at an activity regularly that

conditioning

The start that begins by turning one blade to the side and pushing off.

Picking up speed by continuing side pressure on skate blade.

develops and conditions the body as a whole and is most closely related to what you're going to be playing.

You'd expect a sprinter or a distance runner to do a lot of running, wouldn't you? So why not a lot of skating and hockey-related activities for a hockey player?

Running certainly is a good conditioning method for almost any athlete. I can't think of anything—oh, maybe something offbeat like arm wrestling—in which the legs are not important.

There are other activities that you can do, but I think you have to keep in mind your eventual target. For instance, in some sports a regular weight-lifting program is mandatory. And I don't think a reasonable amount of weight lifting will do a hockey player any harm.

But remember that I said "reasonable." I don't believe that a hockey player, particularly a youngster, should concentrate too much on weight lifting. Some lifting to build up the arms and back, sure. But not too much.

A certain amount of muscle development is fine, but you can get muscle-bound. If you do that, you might be losing the quickness, the ability to make the moves, that is so important in hockey.

A lot of athletes take part in another sport during their off-season months that helps them in their regular or primary sport. So if a hockey player wants to keep in shape and at the same time work on his quickness, he'd be better advised to play tennis rather than a lot of golf.

Mind you, I'm not knocking golf—I like to play the game myself and the swing sure isn't going to hurt my shooting. But if I want to keep or develop my quickness, then I'd be better off on a tennis court than on a golf course.

Any sport or activity has its good points—running, baseball, tennis, golf, soccer. Swimming is super. The Swedes swim constantly and so do the Russians. And you can't knock their success or their physical condition.

I've played against them both and I know that while our styles and methods and rules might differ a whole lot, they're almost always in really prime shape.

All right, let's try to get specific. For a hockey player, and I don't care how old he is, skating is the best activity. In hockey, if you can't skate, you can't play. And that means any level, from the little guys just starting out right up to and including the National Hockey League.

When youngsters come out for a hockey school session, we give them a few minutes of just skating around on their own to get the feel of the ice and start loosening up.

Then we give them ten minutes of routine calisthenics. These consist of pushups, situps, deep kneebends, and standard stretching exercises for both the arms and the legs.

Once everybody is thoroughly loosened up, I like the stops-and-starts routine. I think that is probably the most important drill anybody, particularly a youngster, can do.

conditioning

Let's start at the beginning: taking off from a standing position. There are two ways of doing this and there are different theories on how it should be done. One is to kind of run on the tips of your skates, on tiptoe, to get started much as a figure skater would. The other theory is to dig in with the full blade of your skate, to turn your foot at an angle and push off on the edges of your blades.

Personally, I prefer the method of turning to the side just a little bit and sort of bouncing on your toes.

I don't particularly care for the other method because to me it puts a whole lot of heavy stress on muscles that you don't ordinarily use that much. And that creates the danger of muscle pulls—a major problem area for a hockey player or any athlete.

In other words, I like the method of starting off by running on your toes because to me it is the more natural and normal of the two.

Okay, now we've got you started by whichever method you prefer and use. The next problem is to get you stopped. The idea is to learn how to stop both ways, on either skate. A lot of kids get into the habit of stopping in just one direction because it's just the natural thing to do.

For instance, a left-handed hockey player like me turns to his left better than he turns to his right. A lot of kids will only learn to stop in their natural direction. They have to learn how to do it in both directions because a particular situation on the ice and in a game might make it necessary to stop on your off side.

We've discussed starting and stopping, so let's get to the middle—what you do in between as a method both of skating and conditioning.

I think crossovers are very important. That's the skating motion you use when you're skating the corners, making a power turn instead of coasting in a circle.

Young skaters just starting out have a natural tendency to glide or coast around corners. But you can't do that in hockey, you've got to learn to skate the corners. And that's what a crossover is, power skating on your turns.

Now, just what does "crossover" mean? Well, it's a little difficult

Stopping by turning to the side, using the full length of your blade to brake. This should be practiced both to the left and to the right. Learn to lean your full weight into the forward skate, tilting backward to take advantage of the sharp edge of the blade.

conditioning

to describe; if we were on the ice I could show you a lot easier. It is the leg motion you must make to skate, to generate or even maintain your speed, while turning or skating around in a circle.

If you're turning to your left, raise your right leg and cross it over in front of your left leg. You maintain your skating motion, adjusting it to the turn. If you're going to turn to your right, you cross your left leg over in front of the right.

One of the first things I require in my hockey schools is that the kids must skate around in circles. We start them very slowly until I'm sure they have the correct motion down pat.

Here again, it is very important to learn to cross over both to your left and to your right. Game conditions just plain demand that you be able to circle in either direction.

This is perhaps more important to wingers or forwards than anybody else. They're most often cutting over, left to right, right to left.

You start off slowly but learn to increase your speed with practice. So it's a two-way thing, a leg conditioner and a fundamental hockey maneuver.

Another thing I like to have kids do is bounce on their skates, another method of skating through a turn. You hop or jump along, a combination of a racing start and a turning motion.

There are other routine skating drills that are excellent, too, such as lifting your knees up high or even running short distances on your toes. All are important to the development of your leg muscles, which, remember we said before, are primary to becoming a good skater.

The particular drill that I like best, and I think is super for young skaters, is to break back and forth from blue line to blue line as fast and as hard as you can go.

It's important to go full speed from line to line, or longer distances as well. Do the blue-line drill five or six times, relax for a minute or two, maybe skating slowly around the rink, and then go back to the blue-line drill.

This is really outstanding because it gives you a little of everything all at once: starts, stops, speed, stamina—it's all right in there. And you might work on the crossovers as you go around the rink; practice them whenever you can.

The crossover is the skating motion necessary to skate through a corner or turn on the ice. It is also a primary leg conditioning method. . . .

Aim your front skate in the direction of your turn. . . .

conditioning

Lean into the turn, turning your body into the new direction as much as you can. . . .

Lift your back skate, crossing over your front leg in the direction of your turn. . . .

What has now become your back leg is brought forward, stepping farther into the turn. . . .

Now you're back in position to cross over again.

conditioning

The most important thing to remember is not to cut back on conditioning when you're working out. Do it as hard as you can, go full speed as long and as hard as you can and try to increase your speed and distance and time a little bit each time you work out.

If you have energy and time left at the end of a practice or a game, give yourself a little extra. No, I don't mean you should exhaust yourself. I just mean that in conditioning, there is no point in cheating, dogging it, doing less than you know you should.

Always remember to skate as fast and as hard as you can in any drill. Give it all you've got. You're not fooling anybody but yourself if you're coasting, cutting corners in your conditioning or your practice.

In any organized team program, one of the first things your coaches will have you do is carry the puck while you're skating, getting used to controlling it while keeping your head up. That way, you're stick-handling and working on your skating simultaneously.

The pretty standard drill here is for a group of players to line up in one corner and skate to the opposite end of the rink, carrying the puck up and back. Sometimes coaches or other players will pass the puck out in front of you as you start off.

Just remember, however, that if you're keeping your eyes on the puck and not watching where you're going, you are making a mistake.

If you get used to skating with your head down, you're going to do it that way in a game. And that will be a mistake, because you're going to get hit.

Aside from the shock of an unexpected check, the chances are you'll almost certainly lose possession of the puck. And that can mean a goal for the other guys.

So that's the point—do in practice what you should be doing in a game. If you develop good practice habits, you'll be developing a good playing style at the same time.

I like an on-ice practice program to be as varied as possible, to make a conditioning program as interesting and as much fun as you can. For example, take the skating and puck-carrying routine we've just been talking about and introduce a variation. Have two or three

Bouncing or jumping through a turn, using shorter, starting-type skating motions to change your direction.

conditioning

players go at one time, passing the puck back and forth as they go.

What are they accomplishing? They're working on their skating, their puck-carrying, their passing, their timing, and their positioning when they reach the area of the net. All at the same time.

And if there's a goalie in the net, or even if there isn't, the player with possession when he reaches good shooting position can take his shot.

The next obvious variation is to operate with five skaters moving to attack as a group. Then, if you put a defending team on the ice, you're lacking only officiating (particularly for offside calls) from being in a regular scrimmage situation.

We'll talk about rules later, but let's just make the point now that if you practice being onside, nobody crossing the blue line into the offensive zone ahead of the puck, you will be accomplishing something else that will help you in games.

What about when there is no ice available? What do you do then? Well, I think street hockey can be a great help in any number of ways.

When my brother Tony and I were young, we played more street hockey than we did ice hockey. It's obviously what we did in July and August when there wasn't any ice around. I can remember playing it constantly, hours and hours at a time.

You don't need a brother, a group of kids, a rink, or anything like organized teams, either. I remember shooting a tennis ball at a bushel basket by the hour.

I'd shoot as hard as I could from various distances and angles and keep score on myself. I'd take 50 shots at a time to see how many times I could hit it.

When I got my percentage up around 60—hitting the bushel basket six out of ten times—I got a little smaller basket, maybe a quarter the size of the bushel. Then I'd aim for the corners or the edges of the basket and I'd practice and practice until I could hit it quite a few times, too.

What was I accomplishing? Well, certainly I was developing my arms and shoulders and back muscles with the shooting. And I sure did a lot of running, chasing down that ball, particularly when I missed the target.

conditioning

That's part of what you can get out of street hockey. I think skating is important but if ice isn't available, I consider street hockey to be unbelievably important.

You should exercise, concentrate on different areas, according to your needs. But it's always best to have professional advice if you've got a particular problem.

For instance, I remember when I broke my wrist in junior hockey years ago. All that summer I squeezed a rubber ball with my left hand. I did it constantly, to help build up the hand, wrist, and forearm.

You don't necessarily do those things just when you're trying to come back from an injury. In fact, I know some players now who do it to this day.

To tell you the truth, if I could get back into the habit, I should do it, too. I should keep on doing it. It's good for the wrists and the hands and the arms. A habit like that can strengthen you in such a way that you can have a stronger and better shot.

The same thing holds true in off-season activity. If you want to improve your agility and quickness, tennis would probably help you in that area.

But you make your decision on what would be good for you based on your own strengths and weaknesses. And if you don't know what they are, have somebody check you out; your coach or your school physical education instructors would be glad to help, I'm sure.

chapter four

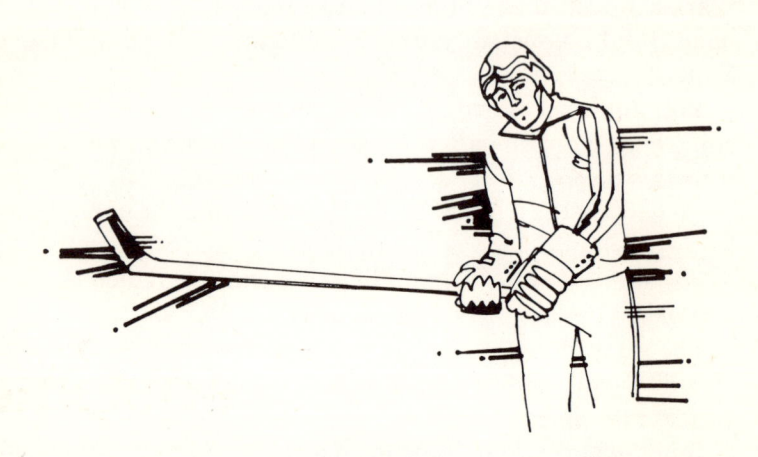

When it comes time to select and fit equipment, the logical place to start is at the bottom, with the most important item—skates.

The proper way to fit skates really depends on the age of the boy. Seven seems to be the age when most youngsters take up hockey seriously. The best starting point is with shoe size, and most kids about seven seem to wear a size one or two.

I consider the Lange skate one of the best you can buy these days. They are as close to normal shoe size as any skate can be. I think in selecting the right size, you should sit the youngster down, put the boot on him, and have him stand up without lacing it.

Check to see if the boy's foot slides back and forth. If it does, frankly I think the skate is too big. And one thing I want to say about that is: it always seems to me to be a mistake to buy skates one or two sizes too big and expect the boy to grow into them.

equipment

You seldom get more than two seasons out of a pair of skates anyway so it seems to me that the original size should be no bigger than an extra pair of thick wool socks will take care of. Then, in the second season, he can discard the extra socks and still have a properly fitting skate for another year.

That's why the Lange skates are good: you can sometimes get two, three, four, or even five years out of them if they fit. And not every boy's feet grow that much.

There is one other thing to be considered when you're trying to get the proper fit. That's the matter of how skates are going to be used.

If a youngster is going to be skating primarily in an indoor rink, a regular pair of wool socks will probably be sufficient. But if he's going to be skating out-of-doors where it is generally colder, then

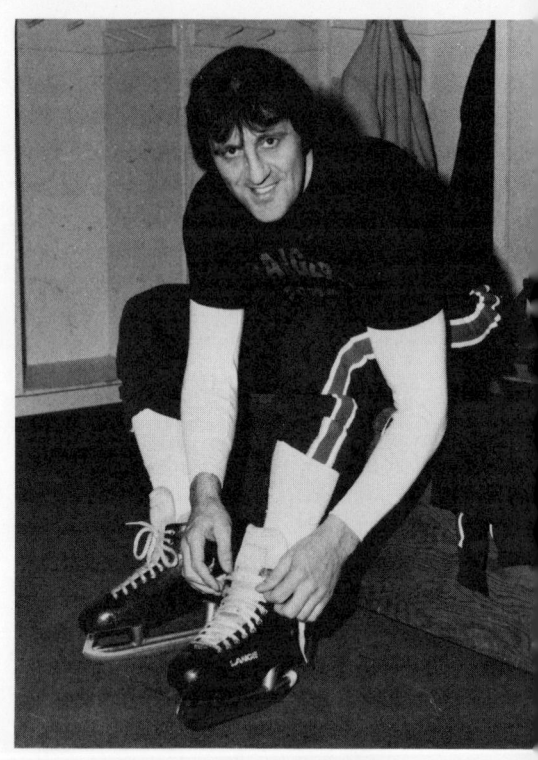

Phil likes his skates laced as tightly as he can stand them without cutting off the circulation. Some players don't lace their skates all the way up. But Phil does, for added ankle support and protection.

he'll probably want to wear an extra pair of insulated socks. So you should take that into consideration when checking the proper fit.

In checking the size, lace the skates up—not too tightly, especially in the lower area, because you can cut off circulation and the foot will get numb.

The top two or three eyelets should be tightened to the point that the youngster feels comfortable. I like to have them as tight as I can stand it, but different people have different preferences.

Bobby Orr doesn't even lace up the top two or three eyelets, and neither does Kenny Hodge. But they're the only two guys I can think

38

equipment

of who don't lace their skates all the way. The majority of players I know lace their skates all the way to the top as tightly as they can stand.

One thing I want to emphasize about skates: I think the tendon guard—the upright section on the back of the skate—and the top of the tongue—the portion that extends above the lacings—should have tape, wrapped around to keep the skate snug.

This provides extra support and protection for the ankles and I think it should always be done. Special wraparound ankle supports are also available.

How much should you pay for skates? Well, I don't believe in buying really cheap skates. If you can afford all the hockey equipment, you can afford good skates.

Skates are, after all, the most important part of your equipment. I hate to see a youngster with the whole outfit—expensive gloves, pads, helmet, and uniform—wearing bad $10 skates.

How do you tell good skates from bad? Price should give you an idea, but there are many other things to look for. An inexpensive skate is made out of split leather or pieces of leather and doesn't usually have an inner leather lining or a good cushion. The cheap skates will have a simple felt pad and the blade will be made of zinc chromate rather than steel. The good skate has a counter or additional support along the sides with extra leather sewn into the back strap portion.

They're getting away from leather soles on skates because they tend to rot out. Cheap skates usually have a vinyl sole and better skates have a surlyn sole and many more rivets for additional strength.

On the cheaper skates, the tongue will be a single piece with a thin felt pad. The better models have a two- or even three-piece tongue that fits over the instep.

Inexpensive skates have what is called the helmeted box toe, made of layers of leather and tar, though they even use cardboard in some instances. The better skates have toes of Cyoclac plastic and are often covered with nylon.

And, finally, the blades on good skates are of high carbon steel. Any decent pair of skates must have tempered steel blades.

Otherwise, they won't hold an edge and will be virtually worthless.

Inexpensive blades will most likely be made of zinc chromate and be nickel-plated. The better or deluxe line of skates will be chrome-coated.

Another way to tell how well made skates are is in the method used to attach the blade to the tubular frame. Inexpensive blades will be welded into place.

You should also check the rivets holding the skate to the bottom of the boot. There will usually be more rivets on the better skates; often one or two of the rivets at the toe and heel of expensive skates will be made of copper.

These are the rivets at the points of maximum stress; the copper rivets are regarded as both stronger and more easily replaced if the skate has to be repaired.

Just buying good, properly fitted skates is the correct starting point, but the skates do have to be cared for. For example, there is the matter of sharpening and how you decide when your skates should be sharpened.

In my experience, it's usually when the blade is stripped—if the blade gets a nick in it—it often loses its edge. It just slides on the ice, it doesn't dig in, and you don't feel secure in your skating. That's when I decide to get my skates done, sometimes between periods of a game and occasionally even during a period of play.

I hold to the theory—my own, really—that I don't like my skates too sharp. I like them so they glide a lot easier. I don't like them done really sharp, with deep hollows in the middle of the blade.

To explain what I mean: the middle of the blade would be sort of concave (curved or rounded inward) and the edges would be extremely sharp.

A lot of professional players like their blades that way, but I just happen to prefer them very smooth, without a deep hollow, just a regular sharpening. Like so many other things, it boils down to what the individual skater happens to prefer, what is most comfortable to him.

But remember, no matter what your preference, your skates do have to be kept sharp. If they're not, you can slip and fall into the boards, risking injury.

equipment

If you see a lot of professional hockey, you'll occasionally see players dragging the edges of their skates on the wooden threshold of the gates onto the ice. Or they'll lay their stick on the ice, hold it with one skate, and drag the other skate across the shaft. I do it quite a bit.

In my case, it's because my skates are too sharp and I don't like them that way. I just tilt my skates and drag the outside edge a little bit. Rubbing it along the wood dulls the blade just a little, to the point that I feel comfortable.

It's again a case of what you want and how you want it. But be sure you don't drag them on a nail or anything metal. If you do, you're going to strip the edge.

I think I'd better explain why I take the very sharp edge off my skates quite often—perhaps more than most other players. I personally believe that the bigger you are the less sharp your skates should be. A big skater with very sharp skates digs deep into the ice. I believe a small or light player should have his skates sharpened a little bit more.

Next are the shin pads. I think the knee portion of the shin pad should fit comfortably over the entire knee, covering over a little bit of the side of the knee. Not too much, because it could hinder movement.

The shin section should extend from just below the knee itself right to the top of the boot or shoe portion of the skate. In other words, it should fit properly, not leaving any gaps at the bottom but still covering the full knee.

The shin pad should consist of both a good, strong plastic front—something strong enough to withstand the pressure of getting hit by a puck—and a comfortable backing or pad of felt.

Shin pads come in just about every price range, and it's not always quite so easy to tell which are the best. I think the quickest way is to check the thickness of the felt pad.

The good ones have a 30-ounce felt backing and the less expensive models have a 24-ounce felt. The knee and shin portions of the good ones are of polyethylene plastic and the best ones have a cloverleaf design top with tendon protection designed to cover the areas at the sides of the knee.

Properly fitted shin pads reach from the top of the skate to the top of the knee.

The pro style have large wraparound wings to cover the sides and even the backs of the calves. The best have a foam cushion under the kneecap and the trend is to a nylon cover because it doesn't soak up perspiration the way felt does.

The inexpensive pads have injection-moulded caps and knee hinges made of vinyl. The better shin guards have match-moulded caps and shin sections of 100-gauge plastic with leather hinges.

Cheap shin pads often have straps for use over jeans in pond hockey, but the better ones do not because they're designed to go under regular uniform stockings.

equipment

I do believe shin pads should always be taped or tightened after you've got your stockings on. I know when we were kids we used a heavy rubber band from an old inner tube. But those things are antiques now and tape will do the job just as well or better. They also have elasticized straps available.

Obviously, the stockings should go over the shin pads, and this brings me to something that bothers me about today's youngsters. A garter belt is absolutely necessary to hold the stockings up and in place. A lot of kids don't want to wear a garter belt for some reason—I guess it's obvious—but you have to wear it. I do and every other pro I know does, too.

It not only makes you look good but it allows you to feel comfortable. Believe me, you'll look silly and feel pretty stupid if your stockings slide down to the tops of the shin pads.

The better garter belts have four elastic drops or straps, allowing two clips for each stocking. The less expensive models have only two drops, one for each side. The better ones are more adjustable, too.

On the subject of hidden accessories, the best suspenders are heavy-duty elastic with a heavy chrome-and-leather harness where the three pieces—the back strap and the two front straps—are joined together at the back. The good ones have adjustable brass hardware and good leather button fasteners.

And just remember, you wouldn't think of playing without suspenders because your pants would fall down. So don't be childish about the garter belt, either.

Then there is the most important piece of protective equipment a boy can wear, the athletic supporter. There is both the inner supporter, which is a matter of comfort, and the outer supporter, the one that holds the cup.

I don't think anybody should ever play hockey, practice hockey, or anything else without wearing this protection. As you know, getting hit in this area can be very painful and potentially very serious.

The supporter is the first thing you put on when you're getting dressed, and I consider this to be significant in terms of its importance.

The inner supporter is pretty much standard; it's the same kind used in almost any athletic activity, and varies a good deal in price depending on material, style, and design.

The outer supporter is different in that it has a pouch or pocket to hold the cup. The size of the cup, and therefore the size of the pocket, varies according to position.

Goalies, of course, wear the largest and heaviest cup. Defensemen generally wear larger cups, sometimes even goalie models, because they're in the line of fire and are often required to block shots.

The larger and better outer supporters have an additional band of foam in the waistband to protect the lower pelvic and abdomen area. The better cups are vinyl-dipped and are encased in a foam edging.

Next in order are the pants. They shouldn't be so big that the player swims in them, and they shouldn't be so tight as to restrict movement in any way.

Just like everything else, they should fit properly to give the protection they were designed to provide. If they don't fit right, the built-in pads won't be in the right places.

They should reach to a point just above the top of the knee portion of the shin pads when the player is standing upright. They should never be so short as to expose part of the thigh.

In trying to determine size, you should try a pair that are four to six sizes larger than your normal waist measurement. If they're the right size, the thigh pads will be directly over the tops of the thighs and the rib pads will be high enough to cover and protect the rib cage.

Of course, the pants should always contain these good protective thigh and rib pads. I think most hockey pants being manufactured now are pretty much standard, but you should never take anything for granted: always examine what you're buying, compare it with other styles to see that it offers full protection.

One thing you might look for in selecting pants is a pad in the middle of the seat to cover the base of the spine. This might be missing from inexpensive pants, but it can be pretty helpful if you fall—and who doesn't?—or get checked against the boards. The top of the line, or pro-style, pants have two additional slash or hip pads in pockets at the outer sides.

equipment

We don't usually have separate rib pads; the tops of the pants provide the normal protection in the rib area. That's another reason why they should fit properly—if they're too small they can leave you unprotected in that area.

That brings us to shoulder pads. The polyethylene caps of the shoulder pads should fit right on your shoulder—not down on your arms or down on the front or back, but right on the top of the shoulder. Again, it's a question of proper fit.

The breast pad portion should extend down over the upper chest area. Shoulder pads vary in design according to position, too. The model designed for defensemen is longer in front, extending down to the tops of the pants. Once again, the job of blocking shots is the reason for the extra protection.

I'd like to stress that aspect of equipment just a bit because of a relatively recent change in hockey. It's called girls. A couple of years ago at one of my hockey schools, we had a number of applications from girls who wanted to learn to play the game.

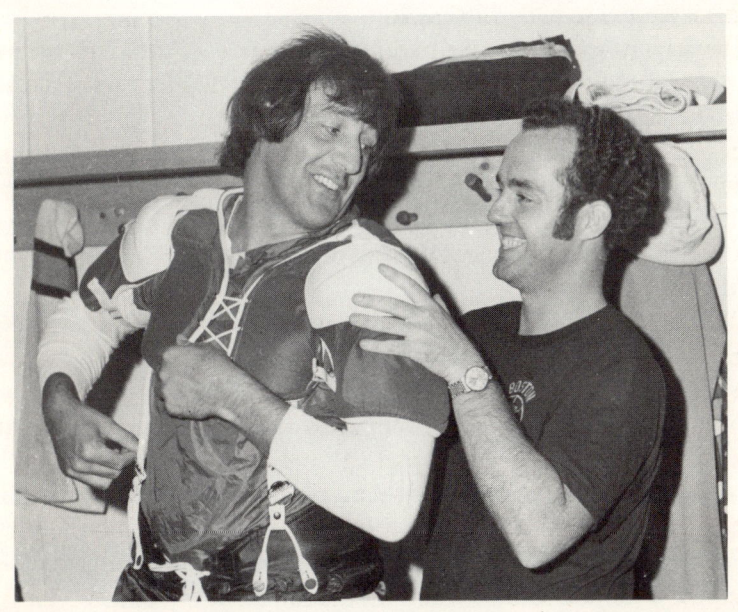

Shoulder pads should fit comfortably not over the top of the shoulder but down over the upper chest.

A flock of them signed up and I want to tell you they worked just as hard as the boys and wanted to learn just as much or even more. One of their problems was equipment tailored to their special needs.

For instance, some of the girls started out wearing goalie body pads for special chest protection. I don't mean that just the goalies were wearing goalie body pads; the forwards and defensewomen—maybe I should call them defensepersons—were wearing goalie body pads, too.

But they found out that the body pads hindered their movements. They soon learned that the shoulder and arm pads designed for defensemen, with the extra-length coverage down the front, gave them the protection they needed.

As I understand it, girls' hockey is growing tremendously and the manufacturers have now started designing and issuing special equipment lines for them.

As a general rule, it pretty closely follows the standard boys' equipment, with a couple of pretty obvious exceptions. The defenseman's chest pad was the key.

The variations are slight for the most part—somewhat different sizing, and so forth. They're even producing a helmet now that takes girls' longer hair into consideration.

Back to the shoulder pads: the upper arm, the outer side, is protected by the arm pad. It should reach right to the elbow, not over it. It should be firm around the bicep, not too tight but not so loose that it can flop around or slide. Of course, the jersey or sweater will help hold it in place.

I know I keep saying everything is important, but it's true. Everything is designed to protect some vital area, and the elbow pads are just as important as anything else.

A lot of kids play without shoulder pads or elbow pads, but I think this is a mistake. A shoulder pad can help prevent a broken collarbone or a shoulder separation. And if you don't wear elbow pads, you can very easily fall on an elbow and wind up with bone chips.

Right now, that may not seem very serious to the youngsters. But an elbow injury now can cause a lot of trouble later on, when they get older.

equipment

Bone chips in the elbow can prevent you from doing any number of things—throwing a baseball, playing tennis, bowling, almost any activity that puts any stress on the elbow.

There's a little doughnut-shaped pad inside most good elbow pads, which I like. It's hollowed out and should fit right over the point of the elbow to give it a kind of double protection. The low end of the elbow pad line is all vinyl with foam padding and extra thickness at the point of the elbow.

The better grades are made of foam and polyurethane-coated nylon. In addition, the better models have bigger adjustable center straps to help hold the pads firmly in place without hindering movement.

All the pads are preshaped to assure comfortable fit and maximum elbow protection. The little doughnut I spoke about is usually standard only on the better grades.

Where gloves are concerned, I don't think there are any really bad gloves on the market now, but it's obvious that some are better than others.

As with everything else, it's a matter of protection. And as you probably already know or will soon find out, a hand injury can really be painful. So the more protection you have, the less chance there will be of getting hurt.

The price of gloves varies according to the material used and the way they're made. Inexpensive gloves are made of vinyl with split leather palms and one-piece thumbs.

Better gloves are made of a combination of urethane-coated nylon with two- or three-piece thumbs and top-grain leather or horsehide palms.

Smaller, less expensive gloves have three back rolls, raised protective strip pads across the backs of the hands, and are stuffed with wool. Better gloves have as many as five back rolls and are stuffed with thick polyfoam padding.

Less expensive gloves may not have a cuff roll, a separate circular pad of foam and plastic between the hand portion of the glove and the cuff.

Important points to remember in selecting gloves that are the right size are the length of the cuff and the width of the palm. The

Top-grade hockey gloves protect both the hands and the wrists from painful injuries.

cuff or top portion of the glove is designed to protect the forearm. If it is too long, it will overlap the elbow pad and hinder your stick handling and shooting because of the uncomfortable fit.

If it is too short, a portion of the forearm will be exposed to slash-

equipment

ing injuries. Ideally, the top of the cuff should fit just below the bottom of the elbow pad.

The palms should be snug-fitting when you buy new gloves, particularly in terms of the width. Remember, leather has a tendency to stretch while gloves are being broken in.

If the palm is too wide, you cannot stick-handle properly because the gloves will float on your hands and you won't get the proper feel of the stick.

It's also possible that overlarge gloves could be knocked off your hands when you're being checked and this could leave your hands exposed and subject to injury.

Finally, the palms of better-model gloves are reinforced with an extra layer at the heel and between the thumb and forefinger.

Helmets next. As always, it's up to the individual, but I consider

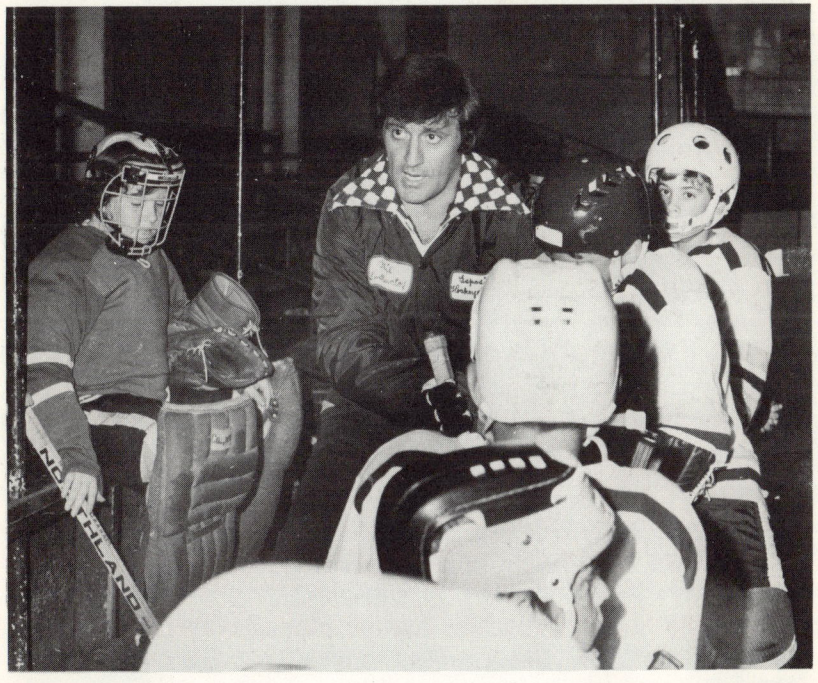

The wire mesh goalie face guard and several of the more popular helmet styles.

the one-piece helmet, such as Stan Mikita wears, to be the best helmet available, the best protection. It is best because it covers all the vital areas of the head and has a built-in suspension system, an adjustable webbing for good fit.

Today's helmets are made of a variety of plastics, such as cycolac, Lexan polycarbonate, and high-density polyethylene. They come in a variety of styles and shapes. Some are one-piece, others are two- and three-piece to be more easily adjusted.

The helmet should protect the head as a whole, particularly the forehead, temples, and the top and back of the skull. The inner padding or suspension web also comes in a variety of styles. One is the web or spider suspension.

Others are the inflatable type, which is filled with air after the helmet is placed on the head, and a model that has a high-density foam padding of various thicknesses. You should really consider carefully all the various styles and types of suspension before purchasing a helmet.

I believe the helmet should be fitted to the youngster, either in a store or a pro shop. Try it on, first for comfort and then to be sure it doesn't wobble around or slip out of proper position.

One other piece of equipment I want to talk about is the mouth guard. There are two quite different kinds, one that fits in your mouth to protect your teeth, and one that you wear on the outside of your mouth.

Personally, I use the formed and fitted inner mouth guard. You do need to be measured by a dentist, but it only costs a few dollars and the end result is much better tooth protection. I've used my present guard for two years and I really like it.

If you do wear the outer mouth guard, try to find one with a little built-in suspension system, inside straps that fit above and below the lips to cushion severe shock but not hinder breathing. These fasten right to the helmet; the chin-strap portion should be substantial enough to hold the helmet firmly in place.

All youth hockey programs require that all players wear mouth guards of some kind at all times. And this is a good rule.

While we're still on the subject of mouth, face, and head protection, there is a fairly new shield on the market that is designed to

equipment

attach directly to the helmet and protect the upper face and eye area from injury. They've done a lot of studies on this and determined that a large number of hockey injuries are cuts in the area of the eyes.

They've had the metal bird-cage type masks, the kind used in lacrosse, on the market for years, but the new device is a moulded shield made of Lexan, a clear material shaped like a little windshield, that fastens to the front of the helmet and extends down over the bridge of the nose.

As I understand it, facial protection is being made mandatory for organized youth hockey programs, so you might be wise to check your local rules before buying a mask that does not meet the specifications.

Most good helmets can be fitted with shields, but again it might be a good idea to make sure it can be attached to the particular helmet model you're selecting for your youngster.

And I must say that I'm personally in favor of anything that will reduce injuries to the face in general and particularly to the area around the eyes.

Now to the proper selection of a hockey stick: this is, to some degree, a question of what comes easily and naturally.

In the first place, to determine whether a youngster is a left- or righthand shooter, you simply hand him a stick and watch how he takes hold of it.

It's just the same as determining whether a boy is a natural left- or right-handed batter in baseball or softball. You hand him the bat, watch the position of his hands, and the side he swings from. That's his natural side.

In hockey, if you're naturally a left-handed shot, as I am, the left hand is down on the shaft of the stick and the right hand is at the top or knob.

Just the reverse is true of a natural right-hand shot: the right hand is down on the shaft and the left is at the top of the stick when you're down in a natural shooting position.

Once you've determined whether the youngster is a left- or right-handed shot, you want to decide on the length of the stick. What I do, in a store for instance, is have the youngster stand at full

51

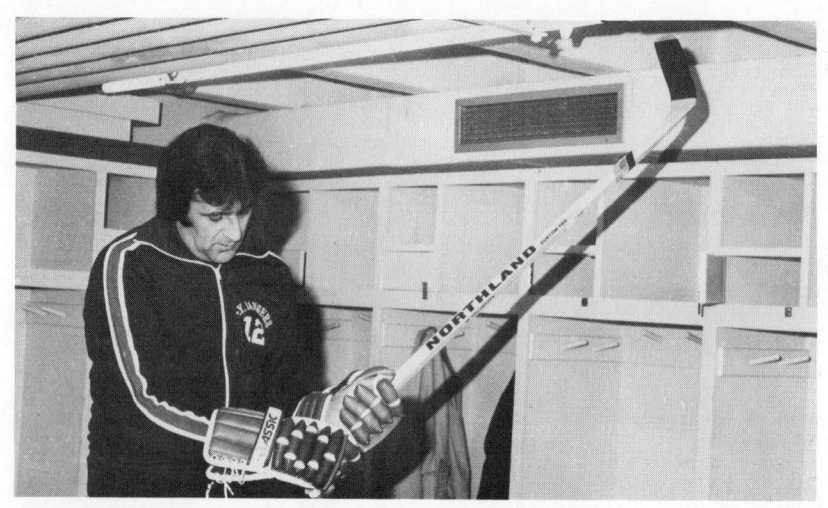

In stick selection, Phil puts his right hand over the knob at the top of the shaft.

Next stop is to select proper length and stick-blade lie.

height and pick a stick that just reaches the bridge of his nose when I hold it upright in front of him.

Then, when he puts on his skates, the top of the shaft will reach just below his nose. That's what I find to be the most comfortable length for me.

equipment

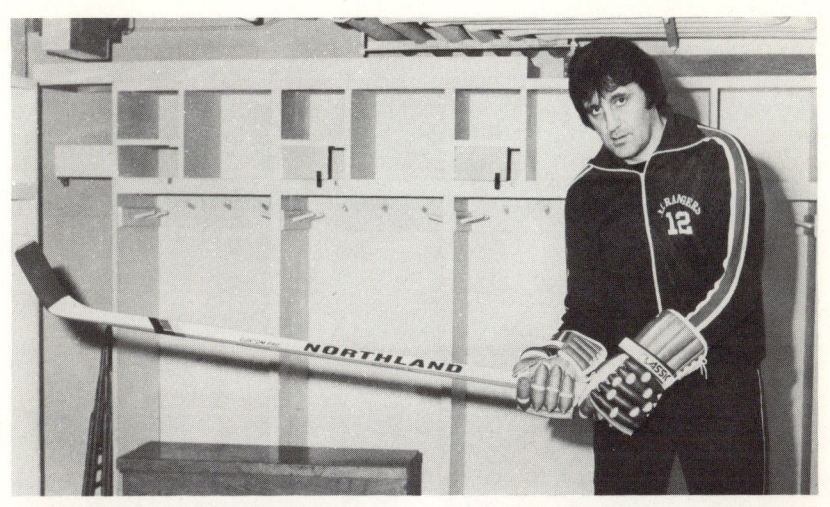

Just reverse the process if you're a right-hand shot.

But, again, the correct lie is determined from a normal stance.

I'm sure that with experience, the length will vary according to the youngster. Some might find they can handle a longer stick more effectively, others might want it a little shorter.

Then there is the question of the "lie" of the stick, the angle of the blade to the shaft. I don't think a young player starting out should get anything higher than a six lie or lower than a five. The full length of the blade should be flat on the floor of the ice when the youngster is in a normal, comfortable position.

I believe that the blade of the stick should be completely covered with tape, because I feel you have better control of the puck with tape than without it. That's my personal preference, although I realize that Bobby Orr doesn't tape his stick. But how many others can you name?

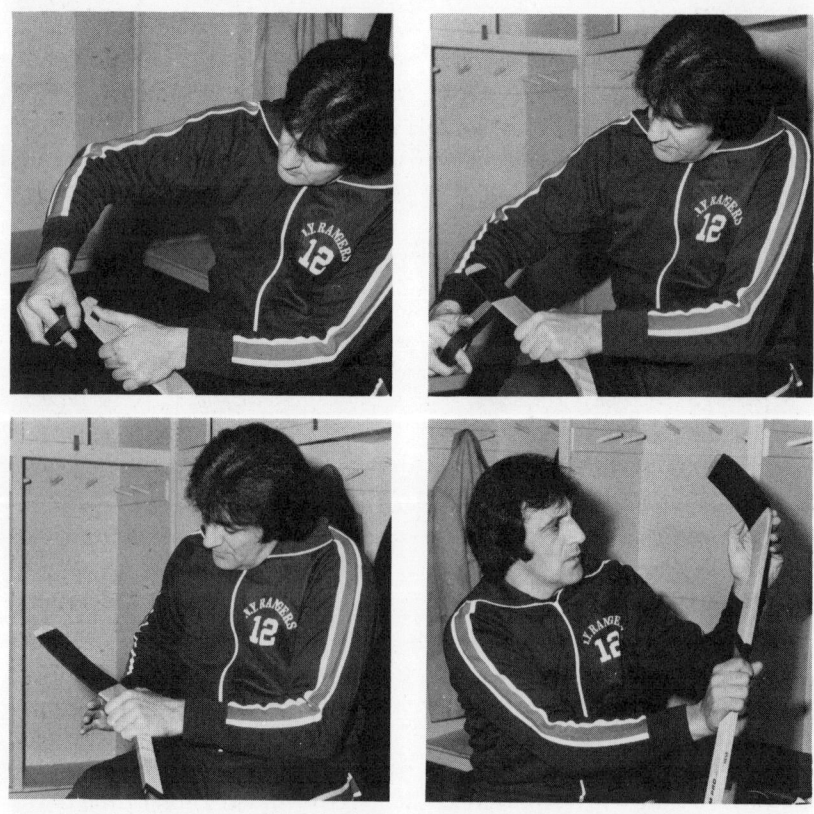

It is a matter of individual preference, but Phil feels he can control the puck better by fully taping the blade of his stick. He notes, however, that some top players prefer little tape.

equipment

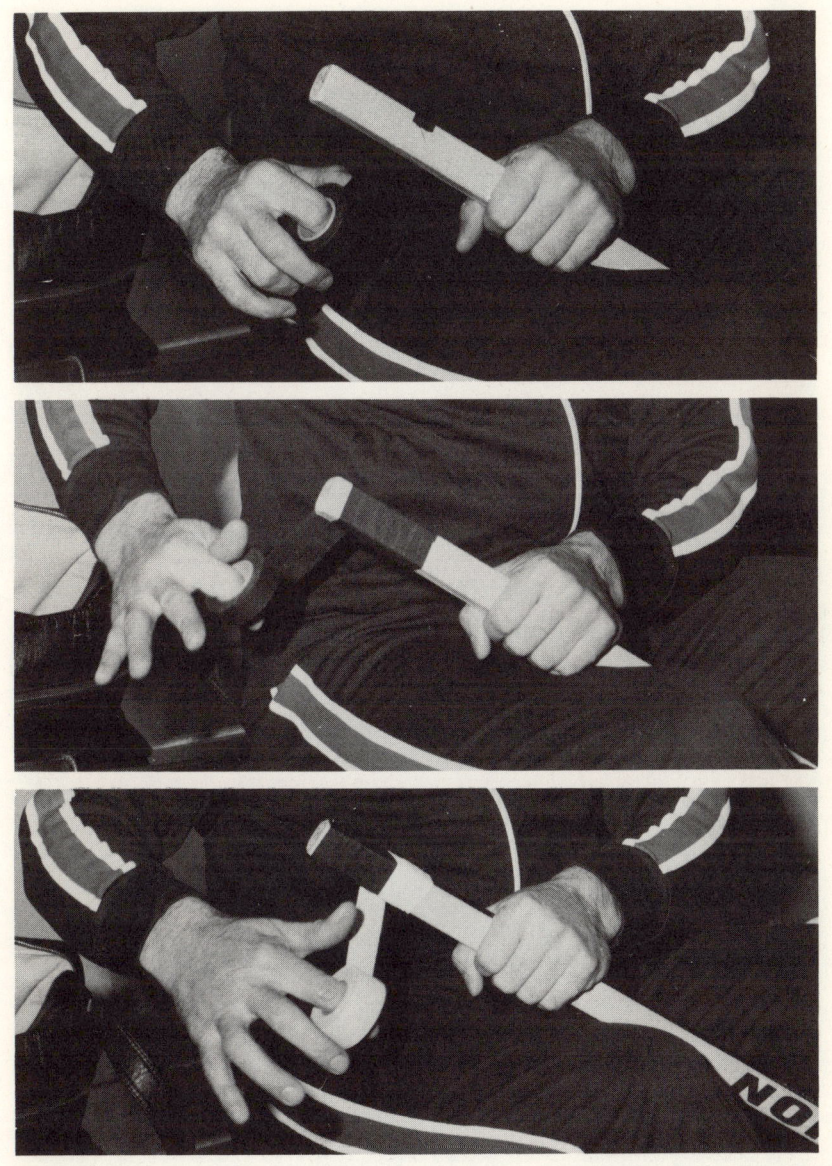

Tape at the top of the shaft just below the knob helps you grip your stick.

Most players prefer sticks with slight curves in the blade, depending on their shooting styles.

equipment

And I don't think a boy should use a big knob at the top of his stick. I feel it should be small enough to fit in the palm of the hockey glove comfortably.

Also, there is the degree of "give" in the shaft of the stick. I use a stick with a firm or stiff shaft. I know a lot of players prefer one that is lighter, has more "whip" or bend to it.

Finally, we come to the matter of the hook or curve in the blade of the stick. If, for example, a youngster is a left-handed shot, personally I don't think it's bad to have a visible hook or curve to the blade so it clearly looks like a left-hand stick.

I know there are people and players who claim the blade should be perfectly straight, but I don't agree with that at all. I think it's an old wives' tale. They say you can't handle the backhand shot, but I don't feel that's true at all.

I'm talking about the degree that we have in the National Hockey League now, limiting the curvature of the blade to one half inch from the heel to the tip of the blade. They check it by putting the stick flat against the wall and measuring out from the wall at the middle or farthest point.

Maybe several years ago, when they permitted the really pronounced hook in the blade, it was difficult to control the puck on the backhand. But that's not true now and I see no reason why a youngster shouldn't have the normal hook or curve in the blade of his stick if he wants it.

And of course it should eventually boil down to what the player wants or feels comfortable with in terms of his stick. If he wants and prefers a perfectly straight blade, fine. It should be up to him and how he feels—and, of course, consistent with the rules of his league.

chapter five

The natural place to start on the actual playing area is with carrying the puck. And in the first place, the best way to carry the puck is with your head up.

If you've got your eyes down on the puck, you're not seeing opportunities to pass or shoot and, most importantly, you're not going to see opposing players.

If you carry the puck with your head down, you're going to get hit. And if you get hit, the chances are you're going to lose possession of the puck.

Some players skate bent over while others skate in more of a stand-up fashion. Remember that if you skate bent over, you should have a lower lie on your stick. If your style is that of a stand-up skater, you should have a higher lie to the blade of your stick. That's why we talked a good deal about the lie of the stick when we dis-

carrying the puck

cussed selection of the stick in the chapter on equipment.

On the matter of the location of the puck on your stick while you're carrying it, here again it is a matter of individual choice. Some players tend to carry the puck near the heel of the blade, others near the toe. I prefer to carry it in the middle of the blade because that's basically where I want it when I shoot and pass.

And I always try to keep it exactly where I'm going to shoot or pass it from, because then I don't need the time to move the puck from one part of the blade to another.

Most of the puck carrying in a hockey game is done when you're bringing the puck out of your own end, moving to the attack. And in that regard, there has been a distinct change in style in the National Hockey League in recent years.

At one time, the center did nearly all of the carrying when a team

60

carrying

was bringing the puck out of its own zone. The defenseman held the puck behind his own net and the centerman picked it up as he circled through.

That still happens some of the time, but more often these days the forecheckers circle with the center allowing and even requiring the defenseman to bring the puck up.

Much of the change came from Bobby Orr. There were a few defensemen years ago who did it quite a bit, players like Pierre Pilote and Red Kelly.

But defensemen are carrying more now because Orr and some others do it so well. In fact, just about every team now has at least one defenseman who can carry it up and really rifle it when he gets out around the red line or his own blue line.

I think right now defensemen are doing most of the carrying from deep in their own zone. Wingmen seldom do it—it is either the defenseman or the center.

The defenseman should carry until he gets just over his own blue line before making a pass or until he reaches the red line before throwing it into the other zone. Or, if he's one of those very mobile defensemen like Orr, he can keep possession right into the offensive zone.

If the carrier is getting checked too closely or has two men converging on him, he either drops it back to somebody else or makes the pass earlier. Once you've given off the puck, you should immediately head for an open spot or a hole so you'll be free for the return pass.

Much of this would be preliminary to a normal attack but is particularly true for the power play. Before we take that up, however, we have to deal with passing. Passes are like shots—there are a variety of them. The kind of pass you make should depend on the situation, your location on the ice, the distance from the man you're passing to, and the position of the opponents.

I prefer hard passes, as hard as the receiver can handle. In the first

---

Learn to keep your head up when you're skating by doing it regularly in practice.

place, a hard pass gets there quicker, cutting down the chances of interception.

Make sure that you look at your target. A pass isn't much good if it's behind the man or too far ahead of him. But remember that if you look at the man and take your time getting the pass away, you're telegraphing it and somebody is likely to move in and pick it off.

Timing is very important and that's something that has to be worked on constantly by both the passer and the receiver. That's one of the reasons you practice skating as regular lines and regular defensive pairs—to get your timing down by learning the other man's speeds and abilities.

There are times when a soft but firm pass is required. Obviously, there's no point in making a pass a man can't handle. In this respect, passing the puck is just like passing a football. In some circumstances, the quarterback must throw a nice, soft pass. In others, he might have to throw a bullet to make sure it isn't intercepted. So I guess the basic rule is to pass as hard as you can provided the receiver can handle it.

Where direction of your passes is concerned, I believe the basic rule is that everything should be directed forward, in the direction of the net, moving in at all times.

There is one exception—a thing called the drop pass, in which the puck carrier simply gives up control of the puck so a teammate swinging behind him can pick it up while using the passer as a kind of moving screen.

You don't see the drop pass as much as you used to. I think that's because it is a pretty dangerous play unless you really know the men you're playing with.

You have to know your wingers extremely well, and everything has to work to perfection, or you can get into trouble with the drop pass.

If you're going in over the blue line, and you drop the puck and the winger isn't ready or isn't expecting it, the opposing team can get possession and immediately they've gone for a three-on-two break.

I think you should be very, very careful about the drop pass. It will

carrying

work if you've got five men on the ice who are alert and familiar with each other, so familiar that they always know where the others are going to be.

chapter six

There are five basic shots—with what I suppose you'd call variations on most of them. They are: the slap shot, the snap shot, the wrist shot, the backhand shot, and the flip shot.

The slap shot is simple. I think the first thing every kid does when he gets a stick in his hands is to wind up and just slap at the puck. I don't like the slap shot. I don't think you can get any real accuracy with it. I very seldom slap the puck. I prefer to snap it or use the wrist shot.

I suppose, in describing the slap shot, the best way to do it is to compare it to a golf shot. You simply wind up and slap it. I'm not a good enough golfer to know whether the form is the same, but to take a slap shot you bring your arms back to full extension and you come through the puck, snapping your wrists as you hit it.

The problem with the slap shot is that you don't know exactly

shooting

where the puck is going. Most players spend a lot of time slapping the puck but when you come right down to it, they have only about a 35 percent chance of hitting the target. In other words, two out of three are going to miss the spot they're aiming for.

You judge the importance of the slap shot, I believe, by looking at all the great goal scorers and what they do or did. And remember, I'm talking about goal scorers, not just hockey players.

Rocket Richard very seldom slapped the puck. Gordie Howe very seldom slapped the puck. The only top scorer who really slapped the puck a lot was Bobby Hull. And he did it so darned hard he scared everybody.

Bobby Orr takes a lot of slap shots, too, but I don't really think of Bobby as a great goal scorer because of his position as a defenseman. But he's definitely in the category of great hockey players.

For a slap shot, Phil takes a position that he describes as being somewhat similar to a golf shot.

Slap your stick right through the puck to get maximum velocity.

shooting

The slap shot follow-through.

Mickey Redmond is another exception to the rule. He slaps the puck a lot. He's worked years on that shot. But he'll tell you himself

67

The snap shot is a shorter, more controlled version of the slap shot.

that he'll score more goals on the snap shot than he will on the slap shot.

   Now, remember, there is no hard and fast rule. There are times when the slap shot is the best thing you can do. If you're trying to shoot the puck from one spot on the ice to another without trying to be right on a particular target, you let go and slap it.

shooting

Preferences vary, but Phil likes to start the puck on the tip or toe of his blade.

The follow-through is similar to that used in the slap shot.

But as a general rule, you want accuracy in your shooting. Which brings us to the snap shot, the one I use most often. For openers, it is similar to the wrist shot. The difference, as far as I'm concerned, is the position of the puck on the blade of my stick.

With the snap shot, the puck moves on my blade. With the wrist shot, the puck stays in a certain spot on the blade. You turn your wrists and the puck goes.

On the snap shot, I drag the puck from the toe or tip of my blade to the middle of the blade and snap it when it reaches that point. With practice, you can get the snap shot off very quickly, and it should be the faster of the two. That's what I like most about it, the speed you can generate with it.

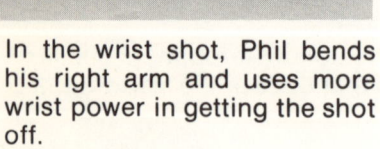

In the wrist shot, Phil bends his right arm and uses more wrist power in getting the shot off.

On the wrist shot, Phil tries to keep the puck centered. (This is unlike the snap shot, in which the puck is moving on his blade.)

There is a difference of opinion on accuracy. A number of players consider the wrist shot the more accurate of the two but in my case it is the snap shot. Like just about everything else, it boils down to what you as an individual are most comfortable with, what you do best.

I prefer the snap shot, and I feel it is the more accurate of the two. But there is room for argument. Each individual must try it for himself to reach his own decision.

Part of my preference is that it is a quicker shot: you snap it off

shooting

Phil uses less arm motion with his wrist shot.

You "snap your wrists" as you get the shot away.

and if you've done it right, it is a fast shot, very tough for a goaltender to stop.

Next is the backhand, the most difficult shot for the goalie. The reason for that is simple: you're not sure yourself where it's going, and neither is he. Sometimes it goes high, sometimes it goes low. It can do almost anything, depending on how you happen to hit it.

The backhand shot is simply the reverse of the more natural shots. I'm a left-handed shot, so to get off a backhander I'll lean on my left leg and lean into it. If I were a right-handed shot, of course I'd lean on my right leg.

The backhander is good when you're going around the outside of

71

The backhand shot is less powerful and less accurate....

a defenseman. You can be holding him off with your body while cutting in on the goaltender.

You just lean into it and snap your wrists as you get the shot away. There's a lot of wrist action on the backhander. It is, in effect, like a wrist shot backhanded.

There are two kinds of flip shot. The one you use most often is the short lift when in close to the net. You use it primarily to lift or flip the puck over the goaltender if he's down or to get it into the top corner.

You're too close to the net for most of the standard shots. You get

shooting

But the goalie doesn't know where it's going, either.

it off best from the toe or front tip of your stick. There's no real speed or power to it: it's just a quick flip to get over an obstruction, such as a downed player or a goalie who has dropped to the ice in anticipation or is crouching low enough that you think you can score over him.

There is another kind of flip, the kind you take from the red line or even your own end. You can be doing either or both of two things, getting it into the zone over an opposing player and/or looking for the tricky bounce that might catch the goalie off guard.

A lot of guys spend a good deal of time practicing the long flip, or

The flip shot is a special thing, for when you want to lift the puck over an obstruction like a goalie.

lift. If you're hoping to beat the goalie with the crazy bounce, it's kind of a change of pace from the slap shot you might otherwise take from a long way out.

The long flip isn't, obviously, a high-percentage shot, but the short flip from in close can be very important to you.

Those are the standard shots. There are really a lot of variations on them. In the final analysis, the idea is to get the puck into the net. If that means a standard or textbook shot, fine.

But it often means a deflection, or something else entirely. Lots of goals are scored by just pushing the puck into the net with the blade of your stick lying flat on the ice.

Let's say, for instance, that the goalie has come out a little way and has gone down to block a shot. If the puck has broken through or

shooting

You just flick it up in the air with a lifting motion.

trickled underneath him, it might be lying loose between the goaltender and an open net.

The idea is to score any way you can, but you should remember that the rules generally don't allow kicking it in. If you do that, you might have wasted a good scoring chance because the referee should rule it "no goal."

I think the word "deflection" is pretty much self-explanatory. That is simply altering the course of a shot, generally from the point, in such a way that the goalie won't have time to adjust to make the save.

As a center, I'm naturally more familiar with one particular section of the ice, the section usually referred to as "the slot," the funnel-shaped area in front of the opponent's goal. Roughly, the slot area is in between the two corner face-off circles. It extends up to 15 feet out from the net in a half circle.

People often ask how I play the slot and, like many other things, I have to answer that it is instinctive. It is one of those things that have to come naturally.

How you play the slot depends on many things, among them: the people you play with, when your wingers pass the puck to you, and how they pass it.

Some wingers pass out, or they center the puck hard and to the front of the net. Others pass more behind the center, more in the direction of the defensemen if the center happens to be tied up by the defense.

So in some instances I play in a little closer, maybe 10 feet from the net. In other instances, I drop back out to the 15-foot semicircle. It will depend both on whom I'm playing with and, sometimes, whom we are playing against. That's another reason for practice—to study, learn, and know the habits of your teammates.

One thing you should know if you're going to play in the slot: it's a tough spot. You take an awful lot of abuse in front of the net, a pretty good pounding.

Just getting into scoring position in the slot can be pretty difficult sometimes. You do it best on a break of some kind, so let's go into that next.

When you hear the words "break" or "breakaway," most people think of a player getting the big pass just at the blue line and breaking in alone on the goalie.

And young players immediately want to know how that's done, how they can set up for a one-man breakaway, to go head-to-head with the goalie.

As a matter of fact, I don't think there is a pattern to it, and if you watch carefully, you'll notice that not even the top professionals get breakaways very often.

The so-called two-on-one or three-on-two break is much more common. Some fans and even some young players get confused by that terminology, but what it amounts to is two forwards carrying the puck in on a single defenseman, or three skaters with possession moving in on two skaters.

shooting

People count the players and they say these plays should be called two-on-two or three-on-three, because the goalie is usually in there.

In hockey, we consider it a break or an advantage if you have a shooter going one-on-one with the goalie while one or two defensemen have to worry about, and even concentrate on, two other skaters. So that's the mathematics of the thing, if you were wondering.

I used the word "screen" in the last chapter in reference to the man who makes the drop pass. But the term is used primarily in hockey in reference to the goalie—screening him or blocking his vision.

Screening the goaltender is just that, trying to block his view of the puck. Some guys are super at it, like Ken Hodge. He just stands in front of the goalie; no particular place except on-line with wherever the puck happens to be at the moment.

The defenseman's job is to get you the heck out of there, clear you away. Sometimes, if you're close to the net, the goalie will take a swipe at you with his stick.

You know that somebody is screening if you see the goalie standing up straight trying to see over the player(s) or bending real low to try and see between the players' legs.

But if he has to move to the side to keep his eye on the puck, then you know that the screen has forced him out of position to some extent and you've got a chance to score as a result.

The defenseman's job is to move people out of the goalie's way, and he has to be careful not to get in the goalie's line of sight in the process. He also has to concentrate on not backing in too close on the goalie, cutting down his maneuvering room.

The most difficult decision is when to shoot and when to pass. That's a decision that varies with each and every play. Sometimes when a scoring chance misfires, you'll hear somebody say there was "one pass too many." And that can be true.

I think that, as a basic rule of thumb, if you have possession and a teammate appears to have a better scoring chance than you do, you pass. But if you have what looks like the best shooting position, take the shot yourself.

chapter seven

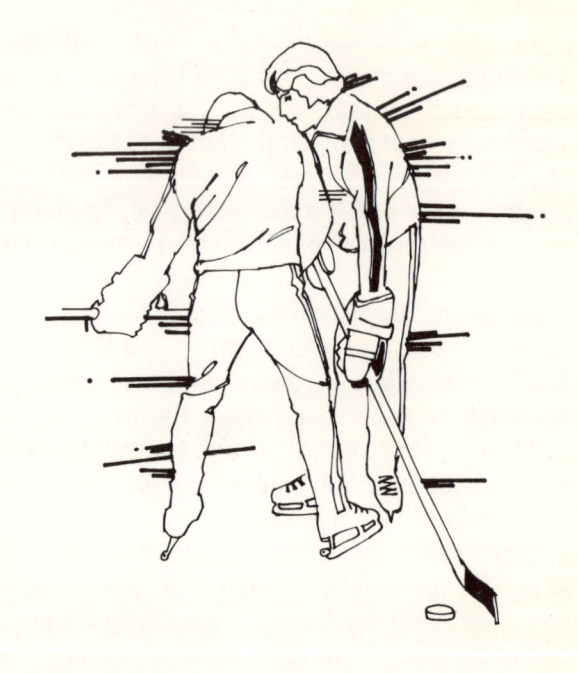

The word *checking* is very important in hockey, but it's a word that many young players misunderstand. When somebody says "checking," many people think only about body checks. Yes, body checking is part of it, but only one part—and not the most important by any means.

Let's start with forechecking—what you do when the other team has the puck and your job is to get possession. If an opponent, say a defenseman, has the puck in his own end and is standing still, I don't like to go straight at him. I believe the best approach is from an angle, to try to force him to move.

If he is around or behind his own net, I like to use that as almost a kind of extra man, to limit him on the moves he can make and the directions in which he can go.

I like to swing in toward him from an angle, forcing him to make a

checking

move. That allows me to swing in front of the net and drive him toward a corner or at least against the boards, using the layout of the rink itself to pin him down a little bit.

The basic idea is to stay on the puck as much as possible. That's your objective, what you want to get. If you can't get the puck, take the body. Use your body to disrupt the man with the puck. This will give your teammates an opportunity to get the puck.

You don't have to hit that hard, that's not necessary. You do have to go into the player and try to force an error. If he can't get a pass off, you or a teammate may be able to get possession.

If you can force him into a hurried or bad pass, it can create the possibility of an interception. And remember, we're talking about forechecking in the other team's end. An interception there can and often does lead to a quick goal.

Standard body check. It's legal if the man you're hitting has the puck. But it could be interference if he doesn't have possession.

checking

After you've hit the man and shaken the puck loose, you break for the puck, or—if a teammate has possession—you break for the net for a pass or a tip-in or a rebound.

In this order, you go for the puck, go for the body, go for the puck, go for the net, and go for the goal. That's your objective and your job.

Now, on back checking, there are different areas and assignments. But you should remember that back checking is important, very important.

It takes concentration and determination to back check properly. I consider it the most difficult part of the game because it requires a total effort to get back after you've given a total effort to move the puck into the offensive zone.

For some reason, it always seems easier to go with the puck into the other team's end. But you have to really push yourself to get back, to help prevent the goal that could offset an offensive effort.

I think back checking best emphasizes the teamwork aspect of hockey. If you're a forward, your objective is to score. But you're just as responsible as the defenseman and the goaltender for preventing the other team from scoring. And dedicated back checking is as important to good defense as anything else you can name.

If you're a wingman, you're coming back on a man who might not have the puck. You have to keep an eye on the man and on the puck.

What you do depends to some degree on the situation of the game. But if you're covering the man, you must stay with him all the way, not just to the blue line or something like that.

If you leave him when you get into your own zone to go for the puck or look for a pass, you're leaving him open and uncovered—and that can mean trouble.

On back checking, if you get caught in the other zone and they've gotten possession on a break, you just put your head down and go as hard as you can.

If you can't catch up with the play, you might pick up a trailer, a man following behind the play, or the point man, just as they try a drop pass.

The thing is, you never know how a play is going to develop. And if you haven't come back as hard as you possibly can, you won't be in position to help no matter what happens.

Back checking is very important, and it's one of those areas where conditioning pays off. If you're in good shape, you have the strength and energy and stamina to get back the way you're supposed to, even at the end of your shift or turn on the ice.

Good back checking helps out your defensemen and your goalie as well. It's just not fair to them to let the other team go in on them with a one- or two- or even three-man advantage.

As I said before, back checking is really the most difficult part of the game because it requires that extra effort and the concentration to do it consistently.

A one-way hockey player, a man who doesn't concentrate on back checking, isn't going to help his team enough and he just isn't going to be around long.

You've got to push yourself, come back as hard as you went with the puck to the other end, and be consistent about it. It's darned hard, but it's the thing—the only thing—to do.

In both forechecking and back checking, you play the puck where you can and you take the body when you can't get the puck. I do want to emphasize that you don't have to kill a guy with a body check. Hit him, hit him hard enough to accomplish what you're trying to do. But if you overdo it, you're liable to be taking yourself out of the play as well and that's something you want to avoid.

One of the ways you check is with a sweeping motion with your stick, trying to knock the puck loose or block a pass. It's something that not too many people do very well anymore, but it is a part of the game.

To sweep is to take a big long swing at the puck with your stick. You might try the sweep check in trying to corner a man with the puck, limit his movements and the directions in which he can go with as big a move as you can manage.

What you try to do depends to some degree on the situation in the game, your location on the ice, and the way the other team is set up.

I suppose your ultimate target when the other team has the puck

checking

Use the full length of your stick to poke or sweep the puck loose.

With the sweep check, you sweep your stick around in an arc.

Close the gap as much as you can by using the full length of your stick.

If you've done it right, you've swept the puck loose and have it in the angle of your stick.

checking

Another standard checking routine is to poke the puck loose. . . .

As the term implies, you poke at the carrier's stick rather than sweep at it. . . .

85

The idea is to spoil his possession. . . .

And if you can come away with the puck yourself, so much the better. . . .

would always be to steal it if you can. But if you're in your own end and the other team is setting up, you want to do anything you can to

checking

Now you're in position to shoot or pass, and you don't have to recover from the big sweep-check motion.

break up the play. Your job is first to cover your man, but you want to regain possession if you can.

You must use any weapon you have available—your stick, your body, your skates—anything and everything you can do and use to be effective.

In many ways, the things you do in checking are the same things you do in the corners, trying to take possession of the puck from the man who has it.

If you're in a one-on-one situation, you take the body and hope to shake the puck loose. If you have help, the first man takes the body and the second man takes the puck.

Digging the puck out of the corners and centering it on a scoring try is very important. I've played with some wingmen who are very good at it.

With the Bruins, Wayne Cashman and Ken Hodge and John Bucyk could really dig it out. When Cash and Kenny and I were together, that was a key reason we set a league record for points by a line. Ken Hodge has since been traded to the New York Rangers.

87

chapter eight

I suppose it's to be expected that my thoughts on goalies and goaltending would be biased. In the first place, it's my job to beat the goalie, to score against him.

And in the second place, I think you might forgive me if I happen to think that one particular goalie, named Esposito, is a super player, the very best.

Before we get into goaltending itself, I think we'd better discuss the equipment. If you recall, when we talked about the skaters' equipment, the word *protection* kept coming up.

And if it was of primary importance to skaters, it is even more so where goalies are concerned. The reason is pretty obvious, too. A goalie is a guy facing shots that scientists claim go a hundred miles an hour and even faster.

His job is to keep that puck out of the net however he can. So he

goaltending

needs protection. I know if I ever had to play in the net, I'd want the best of every bit of protection I could get.

In terms of the goalie's equipment, it is basically what the skaters wear, only more so. Just about everything the goalie wears is an oversized version of the regular equipment. But then he puts on another full set of pads as well as a mask, and, more often than not these days, at least a partial helmet to help hold the mask in place.

Where a regular skater normally wears 20 to 25 pounds of equipment, the goaltender's full set of equipment weighs on the average about twice as much, around 40 pounds or more.

Think about that for a minute. Or, better yet, weigh something that you think might be about 40 pounds. Try carrying it around for a while. Try moving quickly while carrying it.

Goalie equipment is similar to that of the other players, but there's more of it for protection. Note the little posts on the skate blade to keep the puck from slipping through.

If you want to go a step further, tie weights to your legs, enough to equal a goalie's special skates and pads. Then try running around for a while, doing bending exercises, getting up and down quickly and repeatedly. That will give you an idea of what a goalie is going through.

Perhaps the best place to start is the most obvious piece of goalie equipment, his pads. These are up to 10 inches wide and vary in length according to the height of the goalie. Standard pro length is 29 to 34 inches.

Naturally, you want the pad to cover the knee when the goalie is in an upright position. But extra length will be heavier and could hinder movement.

Like nearly all equipment, pads range down from the top, or custom-made, professional models. The best of the line are made of top-

goaltending

grade cowhide leather, specially shaped by hand and stuffed with deer hair. And I'll bet you didn't know that.

Lesser grades of pads are stuffed with kapok and are made of a plastic-coated nylon. The low end of the line are made of expanded vinyl. Youngster versions are usually stuffed with wool. Top grades will have a white felt backing, three eighths of an inch thick, and lesser models will have a canvas backing.

A quick determination of the grade of pad can be made from the number of straps on the back. Pro models have seven cowhide straps that are reinforced leather, while boys' pads can have as few as four or even three straps.

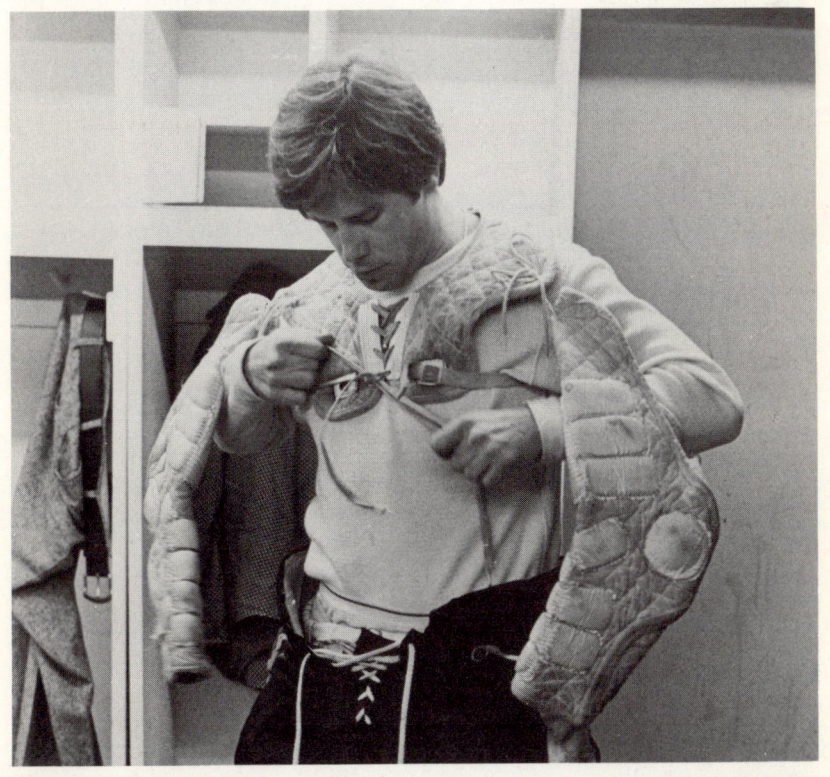

The goalie's shoulder pads cover the outer surfaces of his arms almost to the wrists.

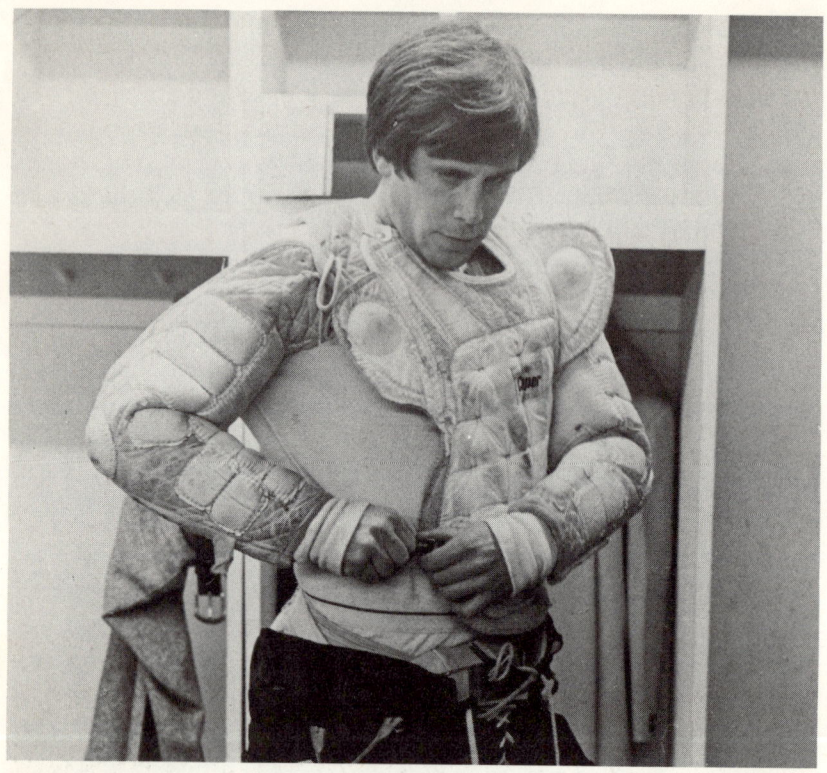

The goalie's chest protector reaches from the front of his shoulder pads to the insert pads in his hockey pants.

Where length and knee coverage are concerned, you can get a separate goalie kneepad that fits right over the kneecap and protects the knee when the goalie is down and the top of the pads have pulled away from the thigh. There's also a light inside leg pad that covers the backs of the calves under the straps of the big front pads.

Next in order would be the goaltender's glove sets, the catching mitt and the stick-hand mitt. And of course these come in both left and right because there are goalies, like my brother, Tony, who are left-handed.

So there will be no confusion, the catching mitt is the big open

goaltending

glove that looks like an oversized first baseman's mitt. The goalie obviously uses that on his catching hand—almost always to smother or pick up the puck.

The stick-hand mitt has a big, flat pad fastened to the back of it

Goalie leg pads fit over the skates and fasten with several straps.

Pads should reach above the knee but not be so high as to interfere with freedom of movement.

because the goalie, in gripping his stick, generally has his hand turned in toward his body.

goaltending

The goalie in full regalia—including catching glove, stick glove, and mask—guards the near corner of his net.

He uses that flat surface to block shots or knock the puck away when it's up in the air in front of him and he can't get his catching glove over in time. That pad, by the way, can't be any bigger than eight inches wide by 16 inches long.

Those gloves usually come in pairs, though you can buy them separately. You can even replace the padding insert if the original gets damaged.

The catching mitt has been changed in the last few years. It used to have a partially open or webbed pocket. Then they went to a "T" arrangement, a leather insert and a heavy piece across the top of the trap.

Now, many top goalies are using a catching mitt that is nearly closed in the trap area. As a result, you don't see so many games stopped while the goalie has his glove repaired.

Under the rules, the goalie can't add any padding or extensions to his gloves or pads that will make them bigger and help him stop more shots better.

He can, however, have special pads or braces to cover or protect an injury or an area where he has a history of getting hurt. He must wear them under his uniform, however.

When this equipment, the gloves and the pads, is new, it takes a while to get it broken in, loosened up the way the goalie wants it.

It's always pretty stiff when you start, so you have to work with it in practice, oil it, and sometimes you'll even see goalies pounding on their pads with a stick to soften them up. And you'll often see goalies wearing new gear in practice but older, comfortable pads and gloves in games.

I'll take up the goalie stick next. It is probably the most valuable weapon the goalie has. You know, of course, that the goalie stick is bigger than the regular hockey stick. You should also know that the goalie is the only one who can continue to play with a broken stick.

When others break their sticks, they have to discard the broken portion and get a replacement as soon as they can so nobody will get hurt on the jagged edge.

Whereas a player's stick blade must be at least two inches wide and not more than three inches, the goalie stick blade is three and one half inches wide. Most players shave their stick blades down to

goaltending

suit themselves, and while goalies may shave theirs a little, it won't be much. They want all the help they can get. It can be, and usually is, 15½ inches long in the blade.

Of course the other major difference is that the goalie stick has a wide portion that extends up the shaft to a height of not more than 24 inches.

Like regular sticks, goalie sticks have varying lies, the angle of the blade to the shaft. I think a young goalie starting out should pick a standard stick rather than a custom pro model. He should work with a standard model long enough to determine his own likes and dislikes.

And in choosing the proper lie, I think he might ask his coach for help. After all, it's obvious that a goalie who tends to stand up straight or is fairly tall will need a different lie from that of a short goalie or one who crouches a lot.

The goalie, remember, wants as much of the blade of his stick as possible to be flat on the ice as often as possible.

The coach is probably in the best position to help the goalie make decisions on his stick, the lie, and the length of the shaft or handle portion.

The coach is in a position to see things about a goalie that others might not notice. So his suggestions, particularly on how much stick a youngster can handle, should help a great deal.

Next stop are the so-called body pads, the stuff a goalie wears that is not immediately visible. The key item is the body pad itself, or chest protector, which really protects the stomach more than anything else.

This is best described as being similar to the baseball catcher's chest protector. They come in varying lengths, with the standard being about 24 inches in length.

Like everything else, body pads come in a variety of materials and nearly all are made to be flexible so they won't hinder the goalie's movements.

They have adjustable straps, of course, and you can obtain additions, such as shoulder-cap extensions that sew onto the upper portion of the body pad to provide extra shoulder protection.

Next are the shoulder and arm pads, which cover the surface of the shoulders, the upper chest, and down over the arms right to the wrists where the cuffs of the gloves overlap.

Most are made of a quilted material, some of heavy felt, which tends to absorb perspiration and become heavier over a period of time. Others are made of coated nylon, which doesn't absorb the sweat.

Usually, the shoulder and arm pads are put on first and the body pad over them. They overlap in the upper chest area to give double protection there.

I should note right here that while most goalies put on their shoulder pads before the body pad, there are some who do it the other way around. And I'm thinking specifically of my brother Tony in that regard.

Like so many things about hockey equipment, what you wear and how you wear it is a matter of personal preference, usually determined over a period of time.

Goalies don't wear the special elbow pads the skaters wear, but the outer section of the arm pad is usually built up and the top pro version has a form of elbow pad built right in.

Here again, if a goalie has a bruise or an injury that needs additional protection, the team trainer can usually devise some special padding to help with the problem.

That pretty much covers the goalie's special body protection. His uniform pants usually have extra-large thigh pads and added protection in the rib area.

As a matter of fact, when a goalie is in position in the net, he should be pretty well covered by special heavy padding from the neck right down to his skates.

Most jerseys or sweaters for goalies come in double extra-large sizes to go comfortably over all that padding and not be so tight as to restrict movement in any way.

The amount of padding and the oversized jersey is why most fans think a lot of top pro goalies are badly overweight. But as a matter of fact, all of them are in top physical condition. They could hardly be carrying around extra weight of their own plus the weight of the pads and still survive in pro hockey.

That brings us to the goalie skate, which is very, very different

goaltending

from the skates used by other players. To begin with, the goaltender's skate is protected by an extrareinforced polyethylene shell on the inside of the instep. It covers the toe and extends to the heel. If you didn't know, you might expect that piece to be fixed to the outer sides of the skates.

But goalies blocking shots with their skates should always use the inner side of the foot, and that's where the extra protection is located. In addition, the bottoms of the leg pads extend down on either side of the boot.

Construction of the inner skate boot itself can be anything from top-grain leather to the new ballistics cut-proof nylon that has been developed. It has extra padding at the top of the ankle both for comfort and for additional protection.

The blades on a goaltender's skates are wider and are sharpened flatter than the skates for forwards and defensemen. The blades themselves have small posts or points extending up from the blade—not quite to the boot—to prevent a puck from getting through. The blades themselves are extra-heavy and are flat, top-high-grade steel without the tubular construction other skates have.

The blade is wider and flatter because the goalie is standing flat on his skates much of the time. It's in large part for comfort as well as for balance.

There's a difference in the sharpening, too. Most goalies don't have their skates ground the way the skaters do and probably don't have their blades sharpened more than once a month.

A lot of goalies will wrap the front of the blade just below the toe to help preserve the toe strap. That's the strap from the bottom of the kneepads, and, where it might get hit quite often they tape over it to help keep it from getting cut and broken.

That brings us to the face mask, and I do want to talk about the face mask in particular because I think people might underestimate its importance.

It has just been in the past few years that goalie face masks have become popular and common. Now almost all goalies wear them and the rules just about everywhere require them. And that's a very good thing.

When we were growing up, masks hadn't been developed to any

great extent. Most of the good masks available today give great protection that goalies years ago just didn't get.

Gerry Cheevers had a habit of drawing marks on his masks indicating the number of cuts and stitches he'd have had on his face if it hadn't been for the mask.

After a while, there just wasn't room left to keep it up. Without the mask, Cheesy or any goalie would have suffered hundreds of facial injuries. They would have kept him out of action and some of them might even have damaged his eyes or ended his career.

So don't ever let anybody knock the goalie's mask, and don't let the goalie on the ice without his mask—not even for practice. You can say the old timers who played without masks were tougher if you want to, but I think the mask makes today's goalies smarter, better, and a whole lot healthier.

As a general rule, there are two kinds of masks: the closed, or molded, style and the wire masks, similar to the face masks worn by baseball catchers and home-plate umpires.

It should be pointed out immediately that most youth hockey coaches and leagues recommend—and often require—the wiremesh masks rather than the molded Fiberglas style worn by the majority of pro goalies.

The reason for that, I believe, is that to give good protection, the molded masks have to be made to order or fitted to the youngster by somebody who knows what he's doing.

If it is necessary, even the protective padding around the edge of a wire-mesh mask is fairly easily adjusted to spread the force of impact over a goalie's face and forehead. But placing the right amount of padding in the right places on a ready-made molded mask is a lot more difficult.

And having one made to order with plaster-cast fittings is a pretty expensive process that professionals can afford. But youngsters and amateurs have trouble coming up with that kind of money.

The stock Fiberglas masks you buy in retail stores usually come with padding that you put in yourself. However, it frequently isn't done right; it isn't done in such a way as to spread and absorb the shock.

The pros go for the molded mask because they claim they get

goaltending

better vision from it and better protection, too. But it has to be properly fitted and padded.

You might have noticed that the Russian goalies wear wire masks. As a matter of fact, I understand they bought some of our masks while they were playing in this country and in Canada.

One of the top Russian goalies wears a wire mask built into a full helmet—which is the maximum protection. As a general rule, that's the best arrangement for youth programs where helmets are required anyway.

The mesh on good, expensive wire masks is made of a strong high-grade steel and is coated in plastic. Such masks also have an adjustable harness. Of course, most youngsters don't need the harness because their masks are fastened right to their helmets. On the pro level, masks are often harnessed to a cranial (or skullcap) piece, which fits on the top back of the head.

You should remember, in all of this discussion about goalie face masks, that in many, many instances young players, regardless of position, already must wear facial protection of some kind or will need to because of rules about to be made shortly.

There are many kinds of facial protection, since safety specifications differ from program to program and country to country and even league to league. So look up your own rules first before making a purchase.

Now, where goaltending itself is concerned, obviously everybody is different; each goalie has a slightly different style with strong points and, conversely, weaknesses.

It's my job as a shooter to avoid, if I can, a goalie's strengths and to work on his shortcomings. Sure, because of the conditions of the moment, I'll sometimes wind up shooting to the glove side of a goalie who is known to be good with the glove. But given my choice, I'll shoot away from it if I can. You have to take what they give you sometimes.

There's always a lot of discussion that some goalies are good standup guys while others are fall-down types who use their bodies more to smother the puck.

I'm not sure I agree with that generalization very much, because all goalies will go down and do it in a hurry if the conditions call for it.

To me, there are other and better ways to differentiate among goaltending styles. For instance, some goalies pretty much stay in the net, waiting for your move or your shot. Others will come out to you, to force you a little and maybe cut down your angle. A lot of

Phil has plenty of shooting room as goalie stays in net.

goaltending

Goalie cuts down on shooting possibilities by coming out to meet the puck and shooter.

people don't seem to understand the idea of reducing the angle, so let me try to explain.

In the first place, most people don't even know the dimensions of the goal. Well, I can tell you that the goal is four feet high and six feet wide. Simple math will tell you that is 24 square feet, but I can tell you that as a shooter, I'm usually aiming that puck for a space 3 inches wide and 1¼ inches high.

That's because under the NHL rules, the puck is one inch thick and three inches in diameter. And all you want is enough space to squeeze it through.

Now, it's obvious that if the goalie stays right in the net, there's some pretty good shooting room. But if he comes out to meet you, it

103

Goalie gives Phil the near corner for angle shot.

But coming out, goalie has cut down the angle, taken away the near side.

goaltending

The same is true from the other angle: goalie gives Phil shooting room.

Goalie approaches, reducing available shooting room.

The closer he gets, the more he cuts down the angle and the smaller the target area becomes.

105

During face-offs, the goalie should be ready at all times.

goaltending

reduces the available target area, particularly if you're coming in on an angle and he's chopping down that angle.

In my opinion, it's really impossible to generalize in classifying goalies, but obviously some are more mobile than others. This is not to say that some goalies don't skate well enough to move around. And let's dwell on that a little bit.

Maybe it was true years ago that the guy who didn't skate very well wound up as the goalie in pickup games. But that can't be true these days.

You remember that we talked about the extra weight a goalie must wear for protection, and how his skates are different from those worn by forwards and defensemen.

But regardless of that, a goalie has to be able to skate, and skate well. In fact, I think he should be able to skate just as well as a forward.

There are lots of times in a game when a goalie has to move away from the net. Sometimes he might even be pushed out of position and have to get back.

When there is a delayed penalty call, it's his job to get off the ice just as quickly as he can to permit the extra skater advantage. A goalie who can't get over to his bench in a hurry can wipe out his team's advantage.

More importantly, however, I like a goalie who can come out to clear the puck or pass it to somebody who is in position to start a breakaway.

A goalie who can skate well becomes in effect an extra man on the ice, and he can help himself tremendously if he can move around, and move around well.

On the individual abilities of a goalie, some of them might go down too quickly, giving you an opportunity to shoot over them. Others might stay up a little too long, giving you a chance to try to shoot under them.

Some don't catch the puck properly, so you go for their glove side when you can. Others don't use the stick well. Gerry Cheevers always had a great stick, one of the best. He really used it.

But every goalie, I don't care how great he is, has a weakness, an

goaltending

area that a scorer should concentrate on. I like to study goalies, looking for the area where I might have the edge.

One thing goalies must remember is that if they do leave the net, it is their own responsibility to get back, to be in position. From a scorer's standpoint, if a goalie gets trapped away from his net, I've got a great scoring opportunity.

The goalie must also be careful not to come out too quickly and too far to meet the shooter and cut down the angle. That's because the shooter can slip a pass to the wing on the opposite side, who would be shooting at an open net.

In connection with that, my brother Tony is a good goalie and one of the best skating goalies I've seen. He has good balance, which is always something you look for in goalies. Tony plays the angles extremely well—that's one of his strong points. If he has a weakness—it's the only one that I find—it is that sometimes he has a tendency to "fall asleep" during the game. By that I mean that when play is in the other end an occasional long shot will beat him.

It's a matter of concentration. He's standing there for 60 minutes or more and there are times when he doesn't get much action. But he's got to keep his concentration to be ready for anything at any time.

So the goaltender has got to be mentally as well as physically sharp. He's got to have strong legs to be able to handle that equipment and still be quick.

Tony has told me, and I've seen it in other goalies, that the extra weight and the down-and-up, down-and-up routine that goalies go through is unbelievably tough on the ligaments. So he's got to be in great shape all the time. And he's got to stay alert all the time, too. It's a pretty difficult combination when you stop to think about it.

In warming up a goaltender before a game, you'll notice that most teams line up near the blue line and throw long shots at him. That's to help him get his timing. I follow the routine of helping him to warm up, let him use all the standard methods without giving him a shot that he might not be ready for. He'll get enough of those in the game.

chapter nine

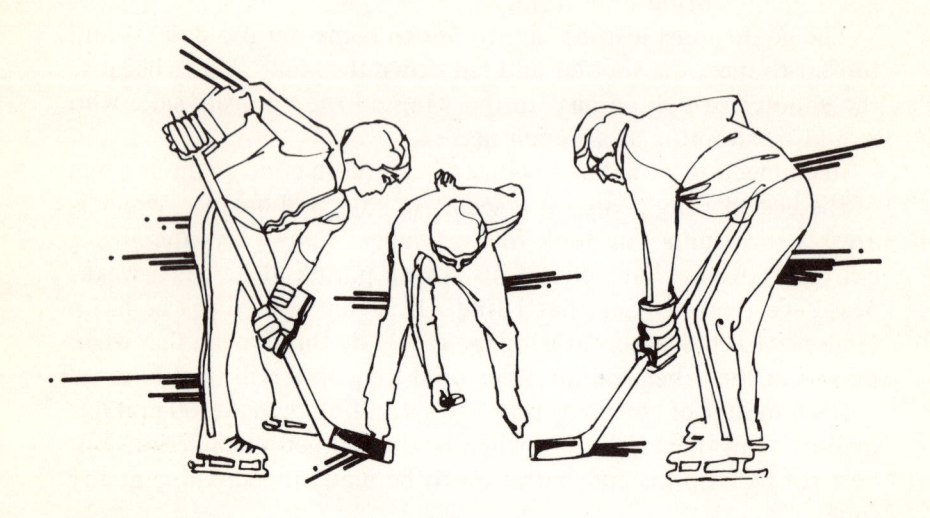

We're going to be talking about power plays and penalty-killing situations in this section, and since both of them begin with a face-off, we'll go into that first.

An awful lot has been written about how to win face-offs, and most of it boils down to one word—cheat. You can try to hide from that word by saying you try to sneak an edge or an advantage.

But there is just no denying it—the player who cheats best wins the most face-offs. Cheating unsuccessfully is why you see so many pros ordered out of the face-off circle by the officials.

It wasn't always the way it is today. Years ago it was very different. But they've passed rules: you have to be back three feet, on the hash mark, and your stick has to be on the spot.

They don't generally enforce the rules exactly, and most officials have differences in their interpretation of the rules, so you try to take advantage.

face-offs

In general, to be as strong as possible on face-offs, I like to choke up on my stick somewhat, slide my right hand (the top hand) down six inches to a foot from the end of the shaft. I like to get right down on my stick for strength and better control of the puck when the official drops it.

I study linesmen to determine their different habits—whether they'll give any kind of a tip-off when they're going to drop it. I have had better success with some than with others and it's usually because of something I've learned in my study.

If I'm drawing on my backhand, I'll put my left foot as close to the center of the hash mark as possible so my knee doesn't get in the way of my stick. If I'm drawing on my forehand, then I try to get my right skate over onto the hash mark so again my knee isn't in my way.

You use different tactics depending on the location of the face-off.

Your job is to win face-offs outright.

Try to anticipate the drop, to be moving with it.

If it is in your own zone, it's a must to win it. When you lose a face-off in your own end, there's the possibility and danger of an immediate goal against you.

face-offs

Start with your hand low on the shaft, then slide it back to normal.

Don't let your face-off opponent tie you up.

Get quickly into position to shoot or pass.

The idea is that if you can't win it outright, spoil it so that your opponent can't either get away a quick shot or get it to somebody else who can take the shot.

If he drops it now, Phil is in position, his opponent is not.

If you can't win the face-off yourself, make sure your opponent doesn't get loose to reach the puck.

In the opponent's zone, you have to try to win the face-off as clearly as possible so you or one of your teammates can have a shot.

face-offs

Knock the puck away, so a teammate can get possession.

If nobody gets possession, go after it yourself.

In the opponent's zone, there are five variations of things you can do to help set up a scoring opportunity.

One is to draw it on your backhand, try to pull it out to the defenseman or point man behind you. Another is to draw it on your forehand, to the other skater behind you.

A third is to push it toward the net and follow it in to take a shot. Fourth is to shoot right from the face-off. Fifth is to shoot it into the corner, where your winger can go after it.

This brings us to the power play, the one really set play in hockey, when you have a one- or two-man advantage over your opponents.

I don't know the exact percentage, but the power play produces many, many goals at all levels of hockey. It's the reason why coaches, when their team is on the power play, will try to get as many of their best shooters onto the ice as possible.

To me, the key to a productive power play is keeping control of the puck in the other team's zone. A lot of teams now throw the puck in and then follow it and fight for possession. I don't like that. I want to carry it in myself or have a teammate do it, retain control while you set up. To me, throwing the puck into the corner is giving up possession and losing a lot of your advantage.

I particularly like the idea of carrying the puck just over the blue line, setting up, and passing it around until you get one really good shot. The Russians are the best example of executing this. They do not waste the puck on the power play. They just pass it around to get one excellent shot on net—not just a good shot but an excellent chance.

Often you'll see that when a team is having trouble with its power play, the reason is that they throw it in and follow instead of keeping possession.

If you watch the Russians play, you'll notice that they don't take many shots on net. They wait for the best shot and they score on it. They keep passing until the defense makes a mistake of some kind, somebody gets out of position, or a man is left open in front.

To me, taking a bad shot, a low-percentage shot, particularly on the power play, is just as bad as throwing it into the corner and trying to follow it in. In my opinion, that amounts to wasting the opportunity. You should never throw the puck away blindly.

You can attribute the Russian success to practice and discipline, but I think the most important thing is their teamwork. They are

face-offs

In opponent's end, try getting a quick shot away.

If you miss, there's always the possibility of a rebound.

constantly working to make every pass perfect, right on the mark, and if they are taking a shot, they want it to produce a goal. They take all the time they need: they show great patience, control, and—that word again—teamwork.

The opposite side of the power play coin is, of course, penalty killing. There are two basic methods and variations of each situation.

I think the ideal situation is to get possession of the puck, get it out to the red line or in the center-ice zone, somewhere outside your own end, and set up a box formation.

That positions your two defensemen near your own blue line and the forwards in the middle zone, passing it around and back to keep possession, killing time in the process.

The other basic method when you have possession is to just throw the puck into the other team's end and follow it in. The clearing shot kills off 10 or 15 seconds, and by the time the opposition gets back into scoring position, they've used up as much as 30 seconds.

That way, you only need four or five clearing passes to kill off a penalty. But that way, too, you always give them possession of the puck, and I don't think that's right. I think you should force them more.

When the other team has possession on the power play, I like the forwards circling into the opposition zone, heading for the puck carrier all the time, circling at him, pinning him down, forcing a hurried pass to set up an interception.

Another method is to pick up a wing and just stay with him. But I don't like that method because it allows them to keep control and move into scoring position. If you're forechecking properly, your defensemen can stand right up, as far out as the red line, again to help force them.

Ideally, you pin them down in their own zone or at least in the middle zone, between the blue lines. And if you have or get possession of the puck, try to get out and stay out of your own end.

If you spend too much time fooling around in your own end, you can lose the puck in too many ways and set up a good scoring opportunity for the opposition. Even bumps or a little rough spot in the ice can cost you possession, and maybe a goal, in your own end.

Once you get possession while you're killing a penalty, try to keep control. Don't take a shot unless you see a good scoring opportunity. Kill off as much of the time as you can in any way you can.

face-offs

I like to rag the puck, circling or pivoting out near the red line, using my body to keep the man away from the puck, and dumping it back to the defense or throwing it into the opposition's corners when I have to.

And of course you always have the option of passing across to your other forward if they make a mistake and leave him open. The pass to an open forward comes up quite a bit because a team on the power play, trying not to waste advantage time, tends to converge on the puck carrier to some degree.

A short-handed goal isn't the end of the world, but it can have a serious effect on a team that was looking to take advantage of a power play opportunity at the time.

chapter ten

We've touched on the play of defensemen in a number of places, but I think we should bring it together a little and perhaps spell it out a little more.

My theory on the key to being a good defenseman is anticipation. Players like Pat Stapleton and Bobby Orr, all those who are great defensemen, have great anticipation.

I don't think defensemen have to be great strong guys. The only time they really use the muscle is when they are clearing guys out from in front of the net. But there are a lot of small defensemen. They're very good at anticipating.

The game has changed to some degree and defensemen have to be good skaters now. They have to be more mobile. No matter where you play you have to skate well. But they are more offensive-minded now than they used to be.

defense: a summary

One of the most difficult jobs for a defenseman, and an area where the anticipation comes in, is on stopping breaks. In a one-on-one situation, he must make sure he takes the body.

The defenseman should never look down at the puck, he should always look right at the carrier's chest. That's the one part of his body he can't move in a fake. If you're watching the puck, he's going to deke his way by you.

If you look down at the puck, he's going to beat you. Make sure you take the body. You don't have to hurt the guy or run him through the boards. You just have to take him out and make sure he doesn't get by you. The puck belongs to the goaltender. That's his job, to stop it. That's the one-on-one situation.

In a two-on-one situation, when they're coming down, the ideal thing is to stay in between them as much as possible, to force the guy

No matter where you are or who has the puck, be ready for anything.

with the puck either to make a bad pass or to go too far into the corner where his angle is too bad and he can't get a real good shot on net.

defense

When you're defending in a one-on-one situation, keep your eye on the man, not on the puck.

He can move the puck around you quicker than you can react.

Now he's in position to beat you.

If you watch the upper part of his body, you won't be faked out of position.

Stay right with your man; if he shoots around you, let the goalie take care of the puck.

Two-on-one is a very difficult play for a defenseman. If you can stay in between the two and force them into an error, you've done the job.

In a three-on-one break, if three guys are coming down on you, there's not much you can do but back in on the goalie, stay in front, and hope that you can intercept a pass or block a shot. A three-on-one is really difficult to stop.

defense

If he loses possession, you've done your job, broken up the play.

Now, go get it and start a play of your own.

Ordinarily, you don't back in on the goalie, but a three-on-one is a very difficult play. The offensive team should always get a shot from a three-on-one for sure.

If the wingmen are covered, the defense should stand up and force a guy to make a play. Move into them before they get too close to the net, before they get set up.

The game has changed, and it's Bobby Orr who has revolutionized it. He made defensemen become more offensive than ever before.

Where skating style is concerned, defensemen have to do what they can do best. They used to have to skate backwards better than anybody. But everybody is an individual.

Orr very seldom skates backwards, but he's the only guy in the league who doesn't do it. Everybody else does. When the guy is coming down on you I think you should turn and skate with him. And as I said before, take the body and never mind the puck. You just have to take the guy out of the play a little bit in order to delay him.

Defensemen right now in this league get more shots on net than they used to or than anybody else does now. That's because the puck goes back to the point and they shoot from there.

When a guy is standing in front of the net, they can cross-check him, knock him down and get away with it. I get it all the time. So the defenseman takes his shot rather than pass to a guy who is getting knocked down.

One of the most difficult and dangerous things for defensemen is blocking shots. That's completely a matter of timing. If you go down too quick, the puck carrier will go around you. If you don't go down quick enough, the puck will go under you or by you before you get down.

There are some great guys in the league on blocking shots, and it's all a matter of timing. You've got to be careful when you're blocking shots. If you don't get that timing down pat you can get one in the face and you can get pretty badly hurt.

Other aspects of defense aren't necessarily limited to the specific job of a defenseman. For instance, there is the matter of individual defensive assignments, a player assigned to stay with an offensive guy. Sometimes it is called shadowing or shadow-checking.

That usually comes from line-matching, where one team will always try to have a particular checking line and a particular checker on the ice when the other club's big scorer or big line is on the ice.

When a player has a specific assignment like that, the idea is to follow a guy around, stay with him, and avoid unnecessary or stupid penalties when you're doing it.

You try to keep the guy away from the puck, and when the puck

defense

gets near him you just check him or check the puck. Those are the most important things.

On the Rangers, we have Walt Tkaczuk, who does it as well as anybody. He follows people around extremely well and stays with them and avoids the penalties.

If a checker or shadow upsets the guy he's working on—makes him conscious of what's happening—he's broken the player's concentration, and that is a large part of his job.

Where line-matching is concerned, as for that juggling act between coaches trying to get a particular line on the ice to oppose a particular player or line, I just don't believe it is worth it.

I know it works, it has worked in the past, but I don't think it should be done. It will probably work in the future, too, but I believe that when you start matching lines, your better players don't get to play as a result. And that's why I don't think much of it.

When a player is coming down on you, I believe it is best to "stand up"; by that I mean it is not wise to back in on your goaltender to the point where a forward will have a great shot from about 15 to 20 feet.

chapter eleven

One of the most difficult things to teach is desire, attitude, mental preparation. And this is as important in peewee hockey as it is in the National Hockey League. I think that what separates the ordinary hockey player from the so-called superstar is attitude—nothing else.

You've got to be right, to be prepared to play this game, to be ready mentally to take all that everybody is going to hand you. That includes opposing players, the media, the fans, and your own teammates sometimes. They're going to dish it out, you've got to take it, and you've got to rise above the abuse.

Remember, playing hockey is a tough life—the travel, the crazy hours, the loneliness. If you're not prepared to take it when you start this game, you're not going to make it big.

If you go on that ice and you're not ready, you're in for trouble. I like to start 15 or 20 minutes, or even a half hour early. Before I go

attitude

out there I concentrate on what I'm doing, what I'm going to do, who I'm playing against, and what strengths and weaknesses their goalie might have.

We play perhaps 80 games, and in maybe five of those games I just won't have it. And when I have a bad game, I blame it on attitude. I wasn't right, I wasn't mentally ready and I wasn't concentrating the way I know I should to be at my best. This tends to confuse people. They think because we don't want to talk that we consider ourselves too important to talk to them. And what we're really doing is getting ready to do our jobs the best way we can.

It's the same situation after a game, especially if we've lost or if we didn't have a particularly good game. We're thinking about the things we did or didn't do and the mistakes we might have made.

We're thinking about everything that happened in the game. This

Today's young players amaze Phil with their ability.

makes the difference between a good hockey player and a mediocre hockey player. But people who aren't players don't understand that.

Attitude carries over to practice, too. Sure, that's work, but not if

attitude

you are in the proper mental state. If you really enjoy playing this game, you can have fun in practice and still do the things you're supposed to do.

To some extent, your attitude is as important to your relationship to your teammates and your coach as it is to yourself. If you're working at the game of hockey, enjoying it, concentrating properly, you're going to get along.

That more or less raises the question of coaching, and that's an area I have considered more and more in the last few years. There was a time when I didn't think about coaching; I didn't think I would want to be that involved when I was through playing.

But I've made up my mind that someday I want to coach. I think now that I would be a good one. I've got so many ideas about coaching that I'd like to try them out.

I'm not going to talk about those ideas now, but there are many, many things that I'd like to try to do as a coach. I've played under a lot of coaches during my career. I don't care to talk about them individually or about their methods. But there were a lot of them and they were all different. Everybody had variations.

I think that if a coach has the right attitude, the right feeling, the right knowledge, and the right way of conveying to his team what it is that he wants, then he has no worries about coaching.

Now, I don't mean that my idea of the perfect coach is one who doesn't have to yell and scream at his players sometimes. There are times when you have to give the players a bad time, there's no question about that. But if you're a smart coach, you can really convey your message without being a mean, mean man. If I can combine all the good things—the best ideas and methods—into one, then I can be a good coach and a good teacher.

Sometimes you hear people say that coaches don't really coach, they just make substitutions, yell at the officials, things like that. I don't agree. I think a coach can make a hockey player play better and thereby create a better hockey team. I think a good coach can definitely coach.

When you're playing on a team, you don't really notice the things you're doing wrong. The coach can see, he can understand, he can make corrections.

More and more now, hockey is getting to be like football with its films—lots and lots of films. You'll notice that a few teams now are getting assistant coaches, another man to see things. Maybe it wouldn't be too bad an idea to let the assistant coach run the team from the bench from time to time and let the head coach sit upstairs. I know it's been done before, and I think that with films to work with, it might be done better. But as I say, those are things I might like to try out on my own before I talk about them.

When I'm coaching I'll be open to suggestions from the players. I've always felt I could and should make suggestions to my coaches. It's gotten me into trouble a few times but I think it's important.

Some coaches will ask for suggestions, others will not. I've always felt that if I had a suggestion that would help the team, I'm man enough to go into the coach's office, close the door, and make the suggestion. The way I've always done it is to say, "Hey, I've got a problem." And we talk it out. I only do that in relation to myself.

If a coach asks about other players, I'll talk about them with him. But unless I'm asked, I will only talk about my own problems. Some coaches I've had would call two or three of us into his office and ask questions, ask for suggestions. And we'd talk about things together.

So my first rule of coaching would be to listen and, if I felt it would help, to ask questions. As the coach, I'd be the one to make the final decisions, however.

That raises the matter of discipline. These days, that's something that has to be self-employed. You've got to take care of yourself, discipline yourself. If you've got the proper attitude, you know what is right and what is wrong, what is good for you and the hockey club, and what is or could be bad.

Because of the players' association, you can't really fine pro players for most things now. You cannot fine a player now for indifferent play or for just plain goofing off. Of course, these are major leaguers I'm talking about. You can sit a player down but that doesn't usually accomplish much.

When I first broke in, a player could be fined for almost anything. I never thought that was right, anyway. I felt the bad part of that was

attitude

Phil hopes to do some coaching when his playing days are over.

that if a coach didn't like you, or he was mad at you that morning, he could take money away from you.

So on the whole, I think the players should be self-disciplined. Oh, maybe a closer check should be kept on the young guys, but that can come from the older players on the team as well as the coach or general manager.

Now, just for the record, I think the players' association is good;

it's helped us with a lot of things in a lot of ways. But discipline is best self-employed.

One of the areas where you as an individual have to make your own decision is in the matter of injuries. When do you play and when do you sit out?

The team doctor can't always make that decision for you. He can't tell how you feel. Basically, if you can skate and can walk, you can play.

Partly, you have to be able to help your team. And here comes that business of pride in yourself again, pride in your team, and pride in your game.

I played games when I was with Boston many times when maybe I shouldn't have. But I wanted to play, the coach wanted me to play, the management wanted me to play. So you play, you don't want to miss the game. That's what you get paid for.

When I got to New York, I wanted to play. But I hurt my ankle and I just couldn't play. Desire didn't help me then. As much as I wanted to play, I couldn't.

That's what the fans don't always understand. They get on you because they don't know you're hurt and can't play. Or you're playing when you're still hurt.

Weeks after I started playing in New York, my ankle was still being taped up until it was like a cast. I still wear the knee brace from when I was hurt a few years ago. Johnny Bucyk used to wear a big corset all the time. He had a bad back, but he had pride and he played.

One of the times pride really shows up is when a player is out with an injury and he has to keep himself in the best shape he can in order to strengthen some area that has been weakened because of the injury.

I can tell you because I've seen many players do it and because I've had to do it myself. It's work and pain and determination. But mostly it's pride.

It's part of that loneliness I mentioned, too, because nobody else can do it; they can't help you, you've got to do it yourself. You don't go around telling friends or writers or radio men that you're hurting so they'll understand. You just go out and do the best you can.

appendix I:
the career of phil esposito

Philip Anthony Esposito was born in Sault Ste. Marie, Ontario, on February 20, 1942, and a little over a year later was joined by a brother, Anthony, later to become the star goalie of the Chicago Black Hawks.

Phil, or "Espo," played six games with Sault Ste. Marie in 1961-62, and for the next two years was with St. Louis of the Eastern and Central Pro Hockey Leagues.

He had 90 goals in 71 games in his first season, 80 in only 43 games during his second pro year. That short second season was because he was called up to the Black Hawks at the age of 21 to begin what has become a record-shattering career in the National Hockey League.

Phil managed to score 20 or more goals in each of three full seasons with Chicago while playing in the shadow of Bobby Hull.

In 1967, Esposito was traded to the Boston Bruins, the key figure in a major six-player deal that was widely labeled as a steal because of his spectacular successes in Boston.

While with the Bruins, Phil scrawled his name across countless pages of the NHL record book. His most sensational statistics were 76 goals and 152 points scored during the 1970-71 season. Both figures are the top individual one-season efforts in NHL history.

And, for good measure, Phil owns second and third places on the goal list, with 68- and 66-goal seasons and is also runner-up to himself in points with 145 in 1973-74.

He led the league in goals for six straight years, won the Art Ross Trophy for total points in five different seasons, and was named for the Hart Trophy as the league's most valuable player in 1968-69.

He led the Bruins to the Stanley Cup in 1969-70 and again two years later, and has earned all-star selection seven times.

Shortly after he was traded to the New York Rangers late in 1975, Phil moved up to third place on the NHL's all-time goal list. He was closing in, too, on the leaders in the all-time point race.

Phil owns dozens of other records, too, in such areas as goals-per-game average, 40-goal seasons, 50-goal seasons, regular-season and playoff goal and point records, power-play goals, and for his part in both team and line records for goals and points in a season.

appendix II: diagrams

THE RINK

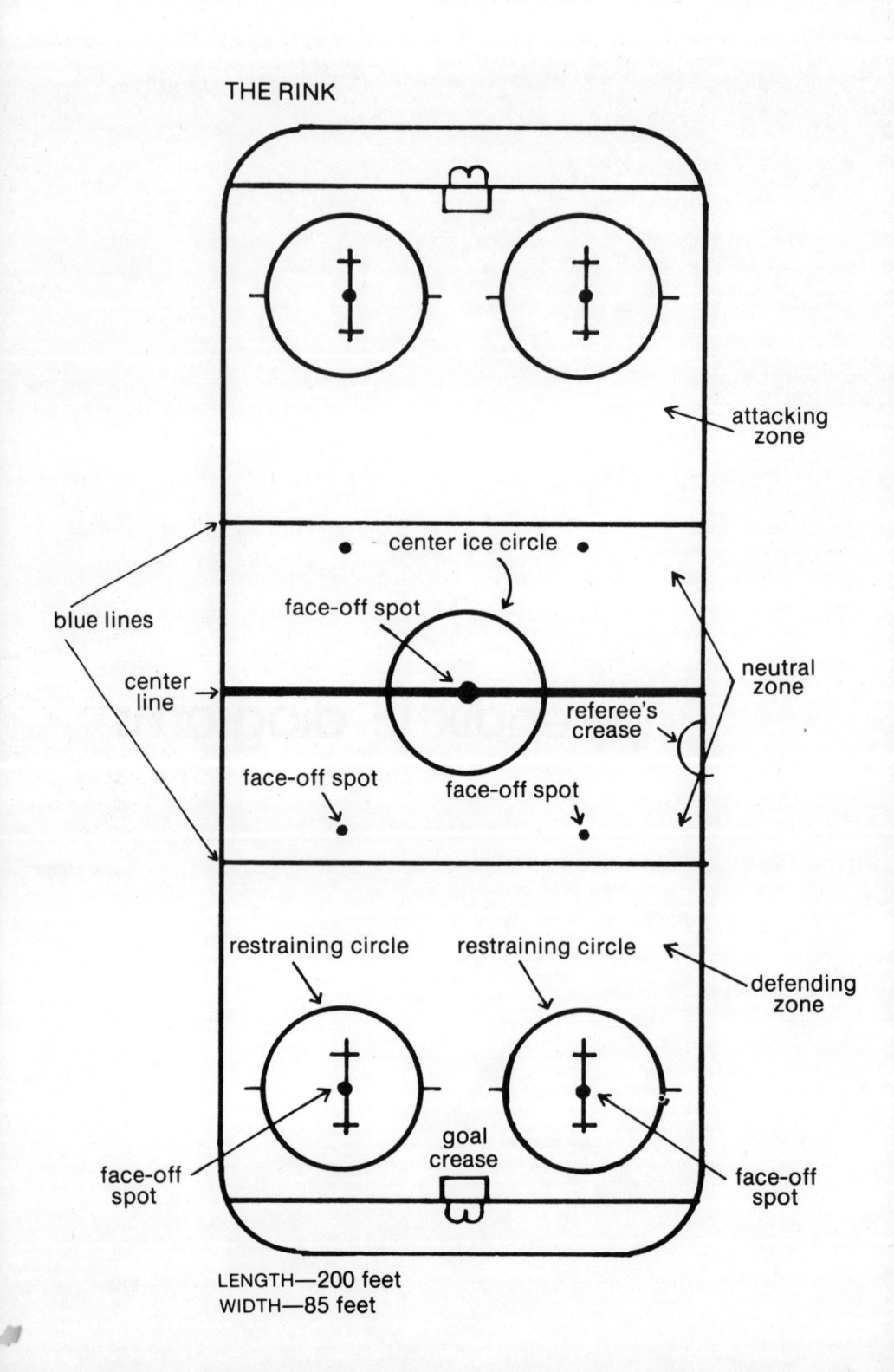

- attacking zone
- blue lines
- center ice circle
- face-off spot
- center line
- referee's crease
- neutral zone
- face-off spot
- face-off spot
- restraining circle
- restraining circle
- defending zone
- face-off spot
- goal crease
- face-off spot

LENGTH—200 feet
WIDTH—85 feet

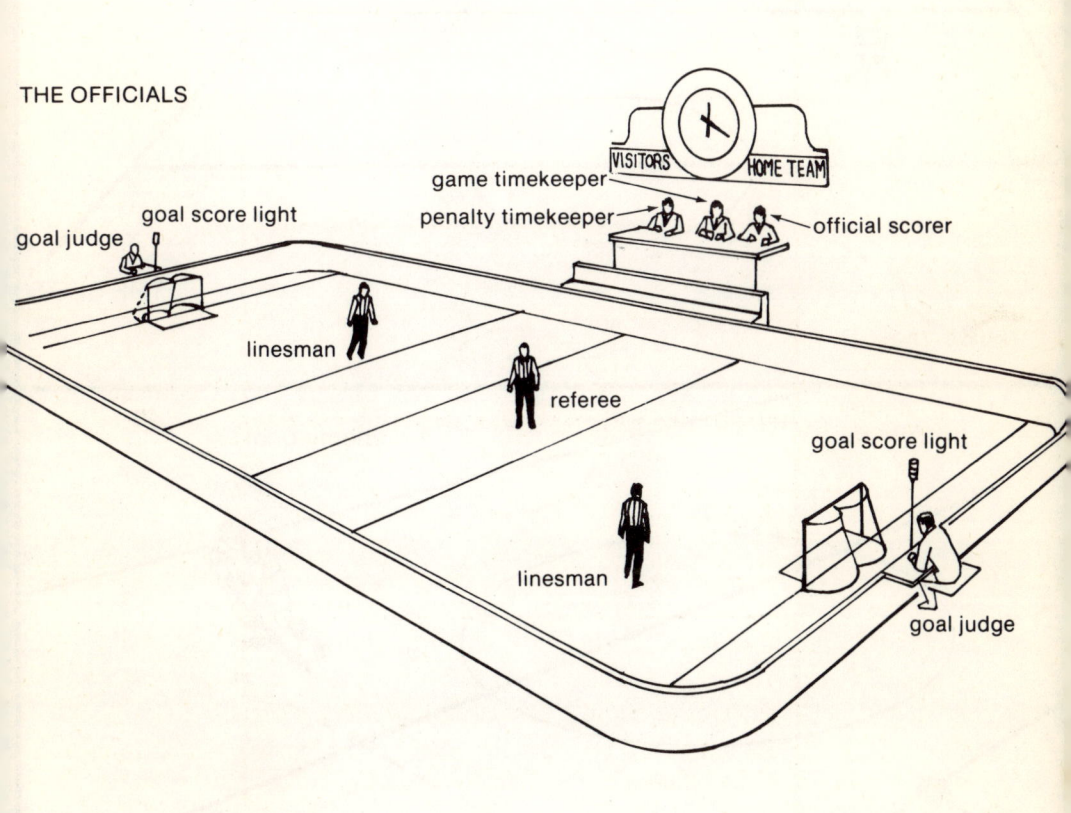

diagrams

THE OFFICIALS

- goal judge
- goal score light
- game timekeeper
- penalty timekeeper
- VISITORS
- HOME TEAM
- official scorer
- linesman
- referee
- linesman
- goal score light
- goal judge

139

Funnel area 15 feet out from goal crease

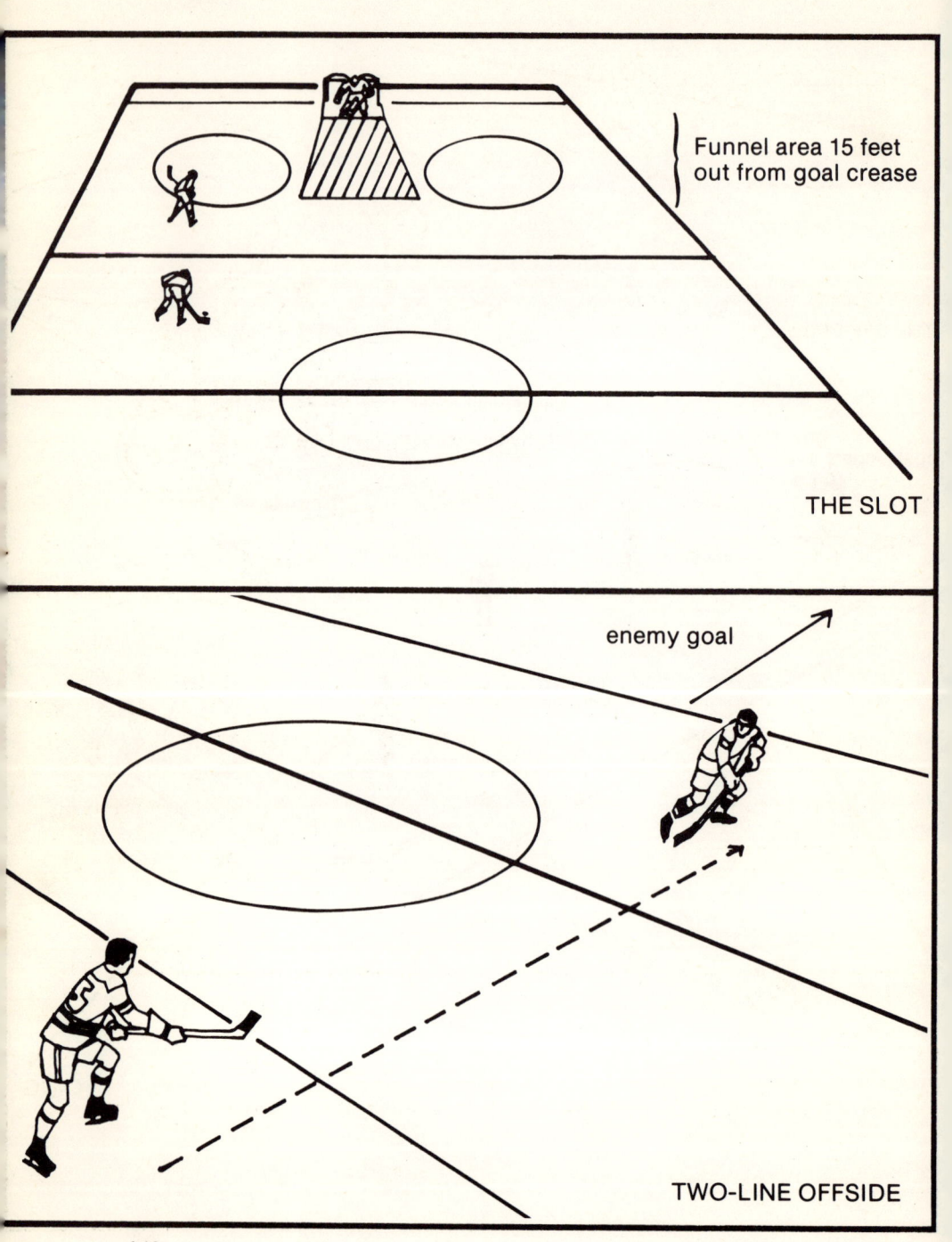

THE SLOT

enemy goal

TWO-LINE OFFSIDE

diagrams

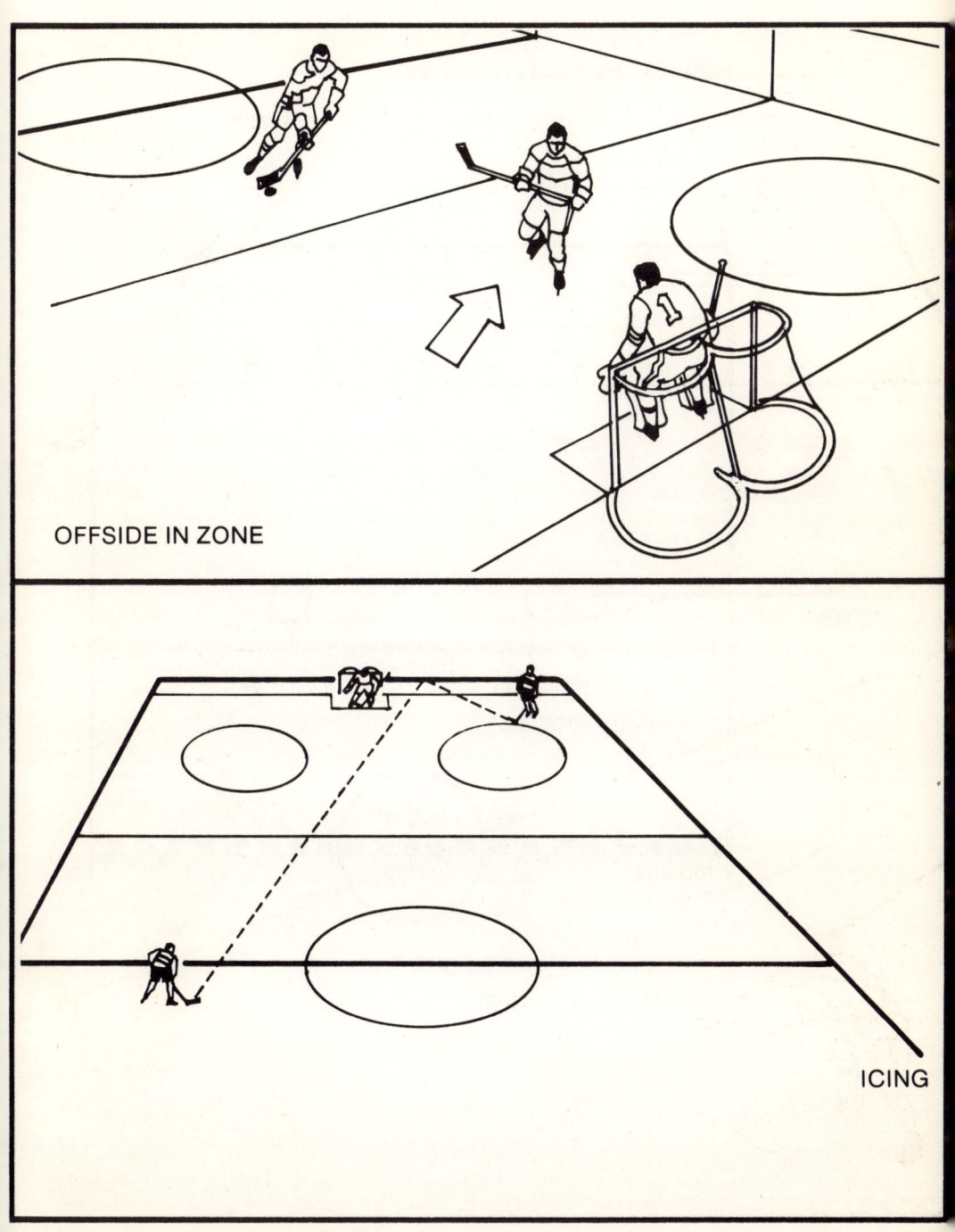

OFFSIDE IN ZONE

ICING

POWER PLAY AND DEFENSE

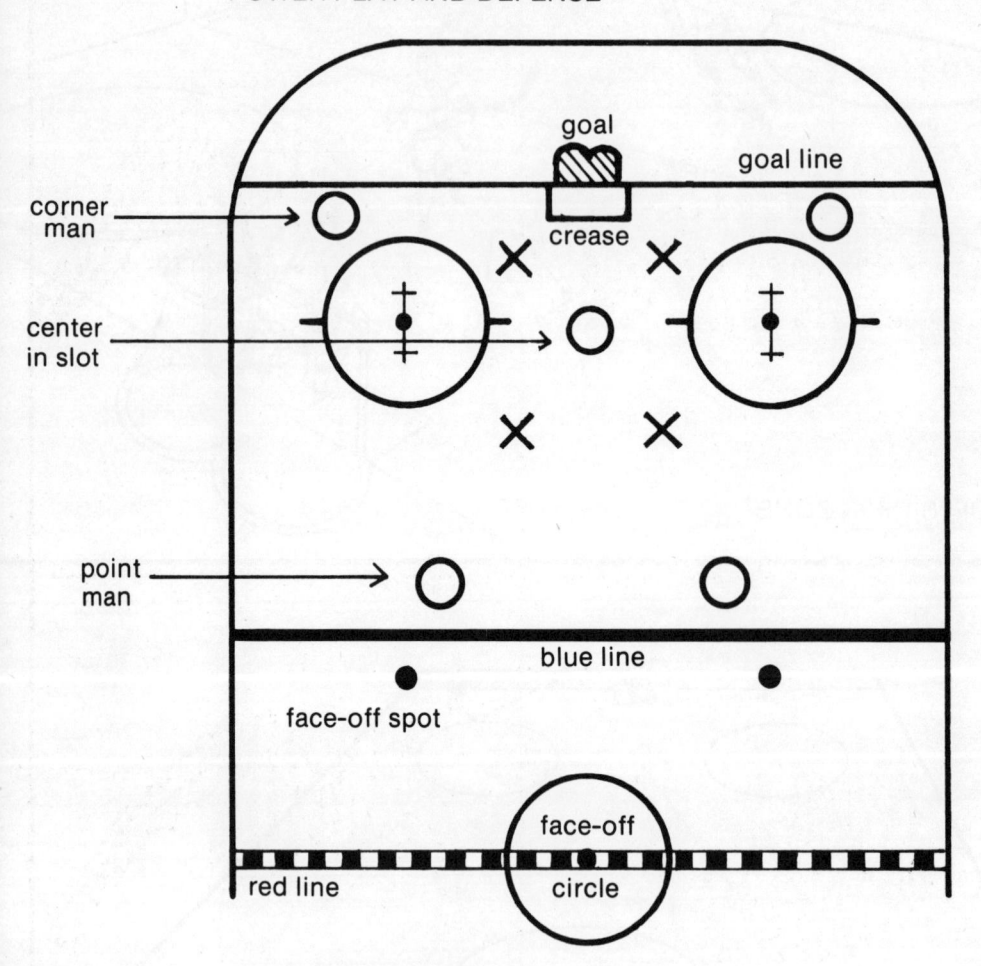

- corner man
- center in slot
- point man
- goal
- crease
- goal line
- blue line
- face-off spot
- face-off circle
- red line

X—PENALTY-KILLING BOX DEFENSE
O—POWER-PLAY OFFENSE

OFFICIALS' SIGNALS

misconduct penalty

washout

hooking

tripping

143

slashing	elbowing
holding	charging

diagrams

boarding

cross-checking

interference

icing

high-sticking

slow whistle

delayed calling of penalty

glossary

Advantage: When a team has one or more players in the penalty box, the opposing team usually has a corresponding player advantage.

Alternate captain: One of the designated alternates to team captain.

Back checking: Returning to your own end to help regain control of the puck from attacking opponents.

Backhand: The off or back side of a player's natural shooting or passing direction.

Bench minor: Two-minute penalty assessed for various infractions (such as too many men on the ice), which is not charged to a particular player.

Blade: Can refer either to the business end of a hockey stick or to the metal edge of the skate.

Blue lines: Lines, 12 inches in width, painted across the rink 60 feet in front of the nets, separating the attacking and defensive zones from the center or neutral zone.

Board check: Use of the boards in conjunction with a body check.

Rules vary throughout hockey as far as board checking is concerned, though it is usually an infraction.

This check is clearly illegal because the victim is not carrying the puck.

And if the boarding isn't plain enough, that elbow is getting a little high, too.

glossary

Boards: The low wall or fence, also called the dasher, between 40 and 48 inches in height, which surrounds the playing surface.

Boot: Generally the upper or shoe portion of the skate. Players often use it in reference to the entire skate.

Breakaway: When one or more players in possession of the puck break into attacking zone ahead of defenders.

Butt-ending: Rule infraction involving use of upper or shaft end of stick to jab an opposing player.

Buzzer: Signal, sometimes a bell, used to indicate the end of a period or stoppage in play.

Cage: A word widely used in reference to the goal.

Carrier: A word often used to describe the player in possession of the puck.

Catching glove: The mitt, similar to a first baseman's mitt in baseball, worn by the goalie on his "catching hand."

Charging: Penalty, usually minor, for running or jumping into an opponent.

Circle: The circular line with a radius of 15 feet around the face-off spots at center ice and in each zone.

Clearing: Knocking the puck away from your own net. Also used to describe a rink-length non-icing pass during penalty situation.

Crease: Area four feet by eight feet immediately in front of the net.

Crossbar: The pipe connecting the upright posts at the top of the goal.

Cross-check: Penalty, generally minor, for checking with both hands on the stick while no part of the stick is touching the ice.

Crossover: Leg motion used in skating through a turn on the ice.

Cup: The protective insert in the athletic supporter.

Curve: The degree of curvature in the blade of the stick.

Dasher: Common term for boards or fence, used particularly in reference to the top surface as "top of the dasher."

An illegal cross-check. NHL rules say the checker's stick must be touching the ice to legalize the check.

Deflection: Altering the course of the puck either on a shot or a pass.

Deke: To mislead or fake out an opponent; usually performed by the puck carrier.

Delay: Usually used in reference to delay in play; may be punishable by minor penalty if ruled to be deliberate.

Delayed penalty: Signal, one arm raised, given by referee to indicate he will call a penalty after victimized team loses possession of the puck.

Dig: Can refer both to an attempt to remove the puck from a scramble or a corner. Also used in reference to digging in with skates for a fast start.

Draw: Refers to face-off, when the player tries to "draw" the puck out to a teammate.

Drop pass: A blind pass in which the carrier drops or passes the puck behind him to a trailing teammate.

Drop puck: What officials do in a face-off to start play.

Elbowing: Use of elbows to strike, impede, or injure an opposing player. Punishable by penalty.

glossary

Elbowing, another common hockey penalty.

Face-off: The method used to start or resume play, in which an official drops puck between opposing players.

Flip shot: Generally a short shot designed to lift the puck over an obstruction into the net.

Forecheck: The move by a defender into attacking team, generally aimed at puck carrier.

Glass: The transparent protective barrier around the rink above the top of the boards. Usually an unbreakable material, not really glass.

Goalie: The player, invariably wearing special padding, whose assignment is to guard the net.

Goal judge: Minor official positioned behind the net and responsible for signaling scores.

Goal light: Red lamp above and behind each net, used to signal a score.

Goal line: The red line across the mouth of the goal, which extends to the sides of the rink.

Green light: Lamp, immediately next to goal light, used to signal end of a period or stoppage in play.

Hash mark: Three-foot lines marking position of players' skates for face-offs.

Hat trick: Term generally accorded a player who scores three goals in a game.

Heel: The section of a hockey stick where the shaft is joined to the blade.

High sticking: Rule infraction for raising or carrying stick above shoulder level in threatening or dangerous manner.

A high-sticking infraction—striking an opponent with a stick raised above shoulder level.

Holding: Grabbing or impeding opponent to disrupt his play. A rule infraction.

Hooking: Rule infraction for hooking or impeding an opponent with the blade of the hockey stick.

Icing: Shooting the puck across two or more zone lines and across opponent's goal line when teams are skating in equal numbers.

Interference: Punishable offense, for impeding progress of an opponent not in possession of the puck.

glossary

Hooking, an infraction on any level and a most common penalty.

Junior: Term widely used in reference to youth hockey program, primarily in Canada.

Lie: Angle of the blade to the shaft on a hockey stick.

Linesmen: In the NHL, two officials who assist referee and concentrate on the blue lines to detect off-side plays.

Major penalty: Five- or ten-minute penalty, used most often for fighting or other serious rule violations.

Minor penalty: Two-minute sentence for rule violation.

Misconduct: A major penalty in several forms that can be called on any of several violations, including abuse of game officials.

Net: Refers to the goal itself, as well as the string netting.

Passing: Term for exchange of puck from one player to another.

Penalty box: Segregated detention areas for players serving penalties of any kind.

Penalty kill: Term applied to a short-handed team trying to outlast a penalty without permitting a score.

Penalty shot: A free shot awarded to a player against an opposing goaltender without being checked by an opponent.

Point: Generally, the defensemen's position on the power play, just inside the blue line in the attacking zone.

Poke check: Knocking puck loose from an opponent with your stick.

Post: Upright pipe on either side of the goal cage.

Power play: The play of a team skating in a one- or two-man advantage in a penalty situation.

Ragging: Control of puck by an individual, generally circling and preferably in the neutral zone, while attempting to kill off a penalty.

Ragging the puck, keeping your body between the puck and the checker.

Rebound: A shot that falls free after hitting the goalie.

Red line: The center-ice line through the middle of the central face-off circle.

Referee's crease: Half circle at penalty timekeeper's position, which players may not cross while officials are conferring.

Rink: The general term for hockey play area and/or the arena or facility in which it is located.

Screening: Obscuring vision of the goalie during a scoring attempt.

Shadow: A defender closely checking or covering an opponent.

Shift: The time a player, line, or group of skaters are on the ice.

glossary

Short-handed: The condition of a team with a player or players in the penalty box.

Slap shot: A standard hockey shot in which the shooter winds up and hits the puck; generally resembles a golf swing.

Slash: Punishable offense, using the stick to slash or hack at an opponent.

Slot: The funnel-shaped area in front of the goal that is regarded as the primary scoring zone.

Smother: When a goalie or skater falls on puck to remove it from play.

Snap shot: A short, quick shot, generally when the puck is located at the toe or tip of the blade.

Spearing: Punishable offense, for stabbing at an opponent with the blade of the stick.

Stoppage: Any interruption of play.

Street hockey: A game that can be played on any large flat surface other than ice, but using rules, equipment, and style of hockey.

Sweater: Original term for what is now generally called the uniform jersey.

Sweep check: A wide, swinging motion used by a defender in an attempt to dislodge the puck or disrupt an opponent's play.

Tendon guard: A reinforced pad, built into and/or strapped around the tendon area of the ankles.

Third man: A player who intervenes in a dispute between two opponents; a punishable offense.

Tip-in: To alter the course of a shot on net to produce a goal.

Trailer: An attacking player who is following behind the play.

Tripping: Punishable offense, causing an opponent to lose his balance by any means, usually with the stick.

Whip: The degree of flexibility in the shaft of a hockey stick.

Tripping, an infraction. One of the most common hockey penalties.

Wingman: The forwards, left and right, who customarily complete a line while skating with a center.

Wrist shot: A shot involving use of the wrists in a snapping motion.

Zones: The three sections of a rink—offensive, defensive, and center or neutral.

index

A

Advantage, 147
Alternate captain, 147
Amateur hockey, 10-11, 14-16, 153
Ankle support, 39
Anticipation, 120-21
Arm pads, 97-98
Art Ross Trophy, 136
Athletic supporter, 43-44
Attitude, 128-34

B

Back checking, 81-82, 147
Backhand shot, 71-72, 111, 147, *illus.* 72-73
Bench minor, 147
Bird-cage mask, 51
Blocking, 126
Blue line, 148, *illus.* 138
  drill, 27
Board check, 148
Boarding call, *illus.* 145
Boards, 149
Body check, 78, 82, *illus.* 80
Body pads, 97, 98
Boston Bruins, 10, 87, 134, 135-36
Bouncing through turns, 27, *illus.* 32-33
Breakaway, 76-77, 149
Bucyk, John, 87, 134
Butt-ending, 149
Buzzer, 149

C

Cage, 149
Calisthenics, 24
Canadian hockey, 8, 14, 16
Carrier, 149. *See also* Puck carrying
Cashman, Wayne, 87
Catching mitt, 92-93, 95-96, 149, *illus.* 95
Center, 59-61, 75, 76
Center line, 138
Charging, 149, *illus.* 144
Cheating, 110
Checking, 31, 61, 78-87, 127
Cheevers, Gerry, 100, 108
Chest protector, 97, 98, *illus.* 92
Chicago Black Hawks, 135
Circle, 149
Clearing, 118, 149
Clothing, 44, 98
Coaching, 14, 15, 131-33
College hockey, 15-16
Corners, 87
Crease, 149, *illus.* 138
Crossbar, 149
Cross-check, 126, 149, *illus.* 145, 150
Crossover, 149
  drills, 25-27, *illus.* 28-30
Cup, 43-44, 149

D

Dasher, 149
Defenseman, 61, 77, 120-27
  equipment, 44, 45
Deflection, 75, 150
Deke, 150
Delay, 150
Delayed penalty, 108, 150, *illus.* 146
Dig, 150
Discipline, 132-34
Diet, 18

157

Draw, 150
Drills, 24-34
Drop pass, 62-63, 150

E

Elbowing, 150, *illus.* 144, 151
Elbow pads, 46-47, 98
Equipment, 36-57, 88-101. *See also names of equipment as* Face mask
Esposito, Phil, 34, 75, 131, 135-36, *illus.* 52, 66, 69, 70-71, 102, 104, 105, 114, 133
    injuries, 21-22, 35
Esposito, Tony, 12, 34, 88, 92, 98, 109, 135
Exercising, 20-35

F

Face mask, 49-51, 89, 99-101, *illus.* 49, 95
Face-off, 110-19, 151, *illus.* 106-7, 112, 113, 114, 115, 138
Fans, 17, 18, 134
Fighting, 19
Films, 132
Fines, 132-33
Flip shot, 72-74, 151, *illus.* 74-75
Food, 18
Forechecking, 61, 78-81, 82, 118, 151
Forward, 27, 118

G

Garter belt, 43
Glass, 151
Gloves, 47-49, 92-96, *illus.* 48, 95
Goal, 103-8
Goalie, 71, 74-75, 77, 101-9, 151, *illus.* 73, 102, 103-7
    equipment, 44, 88-101, *illus.* 49, 90, 91, 92, 93, 94, 95
Goal judge, 151, *illus.* 139

Goal light, 151, *illus.* 139
Goal line, 151
Green, Ted, 19
Green light, 151

H

Hart Trophy, 136
Hash mark, 152
Hat trick, 152
Heel, 152
Helmet, 46, 49-51, 89, 101, *illus.* 49
Henderson, Paul, 11
High-sticking, 152, *illus.* 146, 152
Hockey, history of, 9-11
Hodge, Kenny, 38, 77, 87
Holding, 152, *illus.* 144
Hooking, 152, *illus.* 143, 153
Howe, Gordie, 65
Hull, Bobby, 65, 135

I

Icing, 19, 152, *illus.* 141, 145
Injuries, 19, 25, 35, 46-47, 51, 96, 98, 100, 134
Interception, 79, 118, *illus.* 80
Interference, 152, *illus.* 145

J

Jersey, 98, 155
Junior hockey, 10-11, 14-16, 153

K

Kelly, Red, 61
Kicking the puck, 75
Kneepad, 92

L

Lange skate, 36, 37
Leg pads, 90-92, 99, *illus.* 93, 94
Lexan face shield, 50-51
Lie, 53-54, 58, 97, 153, *illus.* 52, 53

index

Line-matching, 126, 127
Linesmen, 153, *illus.* 139

M

Meals, 18
Mental attitude, 128-34
Mikita, Stan, 50
Misconduct penalty, 153, *illus.* 143
Molded mask, 100-1
Montreal Canadiens, 10
Mouth guard, 50

N

National Hockey League, 9, 10, 11, 18-19, 57, 59, 136
Net, 153
Neutral zone, *illus.* 138
New York Rangers, 10, 127, 136

O

Officials, *illus.* 139
 signals, *illus.* 143-46
Off-season, 24
Offsides, 15, 34, *illus.* 141
Olympic Games, 10, 11
One-man breakaway, 76, 121, *illus.* 123
Ontario Hockey Association, 14
Orr, Bobby, 38, 54, 61, 65, 120, 125, 126

P

Pacific Coast Hockey Association, 10
Padding. *See type of padding as* Knee pads
Pants, 44
Passing, 61-63, 76, 77, 153
Penalty, 126, 153
 signals, *illus.* 143-46
Penalty box, 153
Penalty kill, 118, 153, *illus.* 142

Penalty shot, 153
Physical conditioning, 20-25
Pilote, Pierre, 61
Players' association, 132, 133-34
Point, 153
Poke check, 154, *illus.* 85-87
Post, 154
Power play, 116-19, 154, *illus.* 117, 142
Practice session, 16-17, 62, 76, 109, 130-31
Professional hockey, 9, 10, 17. *See also* National Hockey League
Puck, 103
Puck-carrying, 58-63, 116
 drill, 31-34

R

Ragging, 119, 154, *illus.* 154
Rebound, 154
Red line, 154
Redmond, Mickey, 67-68
Referee's crease, 154, *illus.* 138
Restraining circle, *illus.* 138
Richard, Rocket, 65
Rib pads, 45
Rink, 12-13, 154, *illus.* 138
Rules, 8, 17, 18-19, 96, 99, 101, 110
Running exercises, 22-23
Russian hockey, 11, 101, 116-17

S

Schedule, 17, 18, 129
Screening, 62, 77, 154
Season, 9, 10, 129
Shack, Eddie, 19
Shadow, 126, 127, 154
Shift, 154
Shin pad, 41-43, *illus.* 42
Shooting, 64-77, 102-8
Short-handed, 155
Shoulder pads, 45, 46, 97-98, *illus.* 45, 91

Signals, *illus.* 143-46
Skates
  blades, 39-40, 99
  goalie's, 98-99, *illus.* 90
  lacing, 38-39
  materials, 39
  pricing, 39
  proper fit, 36-38
  sharpening, 40-41, 99
  tendon guard, 39
Skating, 108, 120, 126, *illus.* 22-23
Slap shot, 64-65, 67, 155, *illus.* 66-67
Slash, 155, *illus.* 144
Slot, 75-76, 155, *illus.* 140
Slow whistle, *illus.* 146
Smother, 155
Snap shot, 68, 69-71, 155, *illus.* 68-69
Socks, 37-38, 43
Spearing, 155
"Stand up," 127
Stanley Cup, 9, 136
Stapleton, Pat, 120
Stick, 51-57
  curve, 57, 149, *illus.* 56
  goalie, 96-97
  length, 51-53, 96-97, *illus.* 52
  lie, 53-54, 58, 97, *illus.* 52, 53
  taping, 54, *illus.* 54, 55
Stick-handling drill, 31-34
Stick-hand mitt, 92, 93-96, *illus.* 95
Stockings, 37-38, 43
Stoppage, 155
Stops-and-starts drill, 24-25, *illus.* 22-23, 26
Street hockey, 34-35, 155
Supporter, 43-44
Suspenders, 43
Sweater, 98, 155
Sweep check, 82, 155, *illus.* 83-84
Swimming exercises, 24

T

Team Canada, 11
Team size, 8
Teamwork, 116-17
Tendon guard, 39, 155
Tennis, 24
Third man, 155
Three-on-one breakaway, 124-25
Three-on-two breakaway, 76-77
Tip-in, 155
Tkaczuk, Walt, 127
Trailer, 155
Training camp, 16-17
Travel, 17-18
Tripping, 155, *illus.* 143, 156
Two-line offside, *illus.* 140
Two-on-one breakaway, 76-77, 121-24

U

Uniform, 44, 98

V

Violence, 19
Vision, 58, 77, *illus.* 60

W

Washout call, *illus.* 132
Weight lifting, 23-24
Whip, 155
Wingman, 27, 61, 62, 76, 87, 156
Wire-mesh mask, 100
Women's hockey, 6-7, 45-46
World Hockey Association, 10, 11
Wrist shot, 64, 69, 70, 156, *illus.* 70-71

Z

Zeidel, Larry, 19
Zone, 156